Born and brought [up in] the early
1970s, by the age of ten, Anjula Devi was grinding
and blending spices to perfection, taught by her
father who was a brilliant and inspirational cook.
Using fresh ingredients from their back garden and
from the market, they invented dishes that drew in
all of their neighbours.

Anjula has made Indian food her career, passing
on the wealth of knowledge accumulated with her
father. She has founded her own cooking school,
demonstrates at BBC Good Food Shows, has
been appointed Brand Ambassador for the world's
largest Indian food company TRS Foods and
created her own brand – 'Route 207'. The brand
is named after the London bus journey which
Anjula and her father used to make to buy spices,
vegetables and fresh fish.

www.anjuladevi.com

SPICE
for LIFE

SPICE *for* LIFE

ANJULA DEVI

CLEARVIEW

CLEARVIEW

Published in 2017 by Clearview Books
22 Clarendon Gardens
London W9 1AZ
www.clearviewbooks.com

A CIP record of the book is available from the British Library.

ISBN: 978-1908337 375

Photography: **Dan Jones**
Design: **Lucy Gowans**
Food stylist: **Emily Ezekiel**
Assistants: **Anna Barnett, Becks Wilkinson**
Production: **Simonne Waud**
Editor: **Catharine Snow**

Printed in Croatia by Zrinski D.D.
Colour reproduction by XY Digital, London

CONTENTS

LETTER TO DAD

Dear Dad,

Spice for Life....

I wanted to write to you in heaven with some wonderful news. Our recipes are now out for the world to see. Hopefully Mum is with you now. Remember when Mum used the last of the cumin seeds for her face mask and we had unexpected guests. I had to race to Sira's our local Indian greengrocer for more TRS cumin seeds. You said that you would give me 10 pence if I ran there and back. I was a pretty fast runner in those days.

I finally found the right publishers for our book. I met with Simonne and Catharine, and told them how you taught me to cook at 8 years old, with me sitting on the kitchen floor with a pestle and mortar which weighed more than I did. You added the spices and I would grind. I still remember you saying "Anjula, the spices need to be coarsely ground, so that people eating our food can identify the taste of each spice".

It's not been an easy journey Dad to get our recipes in print, but I know that you would have been so proud of what we have created. I cried when I saw the front cover, because I knew it's exactly what you would have wanted.

All those years ago in our back garden, experimenting and removing spices that didn't quite work. Adding those that did, creating dishes like the lamb and gooseberry that to this day people still love. It is in the book Dad, along with your potato and rhubarb dish and your 24 hour marinated chicken.

Remember when you sent me to the kitchen to turn the chicken that was marinating in the fridge. You'd say "Anjula we need to give this chicken a lot of TLC. It's the secret ingredient which people have forgotten about". At the time I thought that you were crazy, but now I know how important this secret ingredient is. You'd say "Anjula, never cook when you are upset or angry, it will affect the dish".

Teaching me to make light and round chapattis took a little while, but you said "Anjula you are nearly there, next time they will be round". I think you may have said that to me hundreds of times before they were eventually round.

I still have the Indian rolling board which you made me, your tiffin tin which is now over 60 years old, your spice grinder, the pestle and mortar you gave me on my 10th Birthday (you used Mum's nail polish to write the number 10 on it), the small pan you toasted your spices in - and of course your tablas. You played them whilst you sat in the garden next

to the makeshift hot coal fire which always had something simmering. Somehow you could play and stir at the same time!

Sometimes we would have most of the kids from our neighbours' houses in the back garden, and we would have talent shows. You were the judge and it didn't matter what song anyone chose to sing, because you could still create the beat on those tablas.

You once said to me "one day these spices will be like gold dust in your hands". You were right Dad, they are. Even now, I still use the masala dabba which you made for me.

I'm honoured to be writing this book Dad. Thank you for teaching me everything I know. I will write to you again to let you know what people have said about our recipes.

INTRODUCTION

"Anjula just because we don't have any baking trays, it doesn't mean we can't bake like Mrs Copperfield". That was what my Dad said when he wanted me to show him how my teacher, Mrs Copperfield, had taught me to bake bread. Dad was so impressed with the small loaf that I brought home from school.

The following week, we baked the bread. Our options were to use either Mrs Mayo's Fray Bentos tin or use the empty chickpea tins which we opted for. That was my Dad all over, always thinking outside the box. If we didn't have it, he either made it himself or found an alternative.

This book is based on a precious journey that I took with my Dad, and it mainly happened in our back garden. Quite often nowadays you hear people talking about 'from farm to plate'. I was 8 years old when I first started pulling potatoes from the soil and taking them across to Dad, where he would run them under the outdoor tap and scrape them clean, before cooking up some amazing potatoes to put on top on fresh rotis.

Dad would always make enough food for anyone who happened to enter our garden. This book is not just about cooking great food, but also about how food brings people together. It's about sharing easy recipes and using what I call 'key spices' over and over again, until one day you suddenly notice what cumin tastes like, what mustard seeds bring to your dish and how using cassia bark instead of real cinnamon makes a huge difference.

Most of all you'll learn to become confident and familiar with Indian spices. You'll feel exhilarated eating each dish, because it's loaded with a treasure chest of incredible spices with all their culinary notes; spices which I believe can help to keep us really healthy.

Some of the recipes in this book were originally created by accident and remarkably they are now some of the most popular recipes at my cookery school. Like rhubarb and potato or lamb and gooseberry.

I hope you'll feel inspired to create great Indian food, just like my Dad inspired me all those years ago. We don't have 'curry laws' - if you don't like mustard seeds or you think green cardamoms are not for you, then leave them out. The book has been put together to help you gain the confidence to create your very own special blends of spices, so that with a little practice, you can enjoy your very own Indian food just the way you like it.

SPICE
CUPBOARD

My precious spice dabba, containing key spices - cumin seeds, coriander seeds, turmeric powder, black peppercorns, brown mustard seeds, dry red chillies, Indian bay leaves and cassia bark.

This spice dabba belonged to my Dad, and he gave it to me when I left home. He carved it himself, and I still use it every single day.

SPICES

As a 10 year old, I asked for a large pestle and mortar for my birthday. I remember that my friends Suzy, Gillian, Heidi and Janet all wanted Spirographs (bright and colourful geometric drawing toys) or Charlie's Angel suits.

I was much more interested in crushing and grinding spices. My pestle and mortar duly arrived, and had the number '10' written on the side in Mum's red nail polish.

I was so intrigued by what Dad could create with these intense spices. I used to sit on our black and white squared linoleum kitchen floor for hours grinding and bashing spices for Dad's latest culinary creations.

Whole fish would be stuffed with the coarsely ground spices, along with fresh herbs, garlic, ginger and chillies. I can still recall the crackling, sizzling sound that the fish made as it was fried. It was truly delicious. As I think about the popularity of fast food now, I realise how lucky my siblings and I were to have grown up on an incredible diet of amazing spices and fresh produce.

I can't imagine what I would do without the spice dabba that Dad made for me. I still use it to this day. He believed passionately that you shouldn't roast your spices for too long, rather that teasing them with just a little warmth was all they needed to awaken their magical aromas. He had a fantastic analogy for the spices which are at the heart of great Indian food. He saw them as being like a great piece of music. He would say "Anjula, when you cook make food which will exhilarate. Like music you have to have a base, and then carefully selected melodies and harmonies and like all great music there has to be an amazing finale".

My love of spices continued throughout my teenage years. I found that perfecting these spice blends, not too much of anything and just enough to awaken your taste buds, really is an art.

1979 was the year of the Southall riots. Whilst Southall Broadway, a 5 minute walk from our house, was full of chaos and violence, Dad cooked in the back garden. We ate with our neighbours, practically the whole street - white, black and a few Asians - food pulling cultures together. Dad was determined that our little community on

Northcote Avenue was not going to be affected. I even remember that we made parathas stuffed with the potatoes grown in our back garden, with crushed moongra (Indian radish).

Another vivid and happy childhood memory was The Queen's Silver Jubilee street party in 1977. I was hoping that we'd have Sunblest bread sandwiches and some Iced Gems, but Dad had other ideas. He decided that we were going make aloo parathas – "just three spices Anjula, because there will be plenty of kids who won't be used to the spices". I was mortified. Here I was trying to fit in and Dad wanted to make parathas! I remember thinking that The Queen had probably never eaten a paratha. The whole day was a huge success, with people queueing along the length of the front garden's brick wall that Dad built. People spoke about those parathas for a long time afterwards.

I was intrigued one day when I found a little bowl of cumin seeds in the bathroom. It transpired that Mum used it to make a face mask. She said it helped to keep her skin wrinkle-free. I quickly learned that spices keep you healthy on the inside and on the outside too. Ever since then my beauty regime has been based on spices from my masala dabba. Amazing spice masks made with antioxidant turmeric and cumin rich in vitamin E have kept my skin looking young and wrinkle-free at the tender age of 52.

My Dad used to call our masala box the 'Doctor's surgery'. He used to joke that our masala dabba didn't keep you waiting like they did in those soulless surgeries. There were 8 siblings in our house and only one ever got hospitalised. That was one of my brothers when I managed to give him concussion after throwing a huge beetroot at him.

I'm so pleased that Dad taught all the siblings to cook, it's a life skill that everyone should have. Eating well is so important and eating spices with so many incredible health benefits has certainly helped my family to stay fit and healthy.

Key Spices

INDIAN BAY LEAVES

The Indian bay leaf is very different to the bay leaf grown in other countries. Popular in most Indian cuisine, it is very aromatic. It also possesses medicinal benefits and is known for having anti-inflammatory, anti-bacterial, anti-fungal and diuretic properties.

TURMERIC POWDER

This is one spice you should never overuse as it is very pungent. Use to help combat arthritis, stomach pain, heartburn and a sore throat amongst other ailments.

CUMIN SEEDS

This is the herb to opt for if you are experiencing digestive problems and bloating or as we move into winter and flu season (which I never suffer from) to boost the immune system.

BROWN MUSTARD SEEDS

Now these seeds really pack a punch! They add a real nutty fire and richness to any Indian dish – and most importantly they slow down ageing and help with the menopause.

CORIANDER SEEDS

A great citrus, tangy taste and a key player in good Indian food. If over used it will not dominate other spices. Coriander is high in iron, anti-bacterial properties and is an effective antidote to hay fever.

RED CHILLI FLAKES

Spicy and peppery, chillies boost the taste of dishes without masking their flavours. They contain capsaicin, antioxidants, and vitamin C. Chillies are thought to boost the immune system, stimulate metabolism and to be good for diabetics.

BLACK PEPPERCORNS

The King of Spices. They have a fairly intense heat and should be used carefully. Also a good source of potassium, manganese, iron, vitamins C and K and dietary fibre.

CASSIA BARK

Warm and aromatic with a background of sweetness, a member of the cinnamon family but much more earthy, cassia bark helps to control blood sugar levels and cholesterol.

STAR ANISE

Is often used to flavour slow cooked dishes in Indian cuisine. It has a bold liquorice and lemon flavour, so a little goes a long way. It contains antioxidants, and is thought to help improve digestion, treat flu and to help.with rheumatism.

GREEN CARDAMOM

Green cardamom delivers a real floral, aromatic taste with a hint of eucalyptus almost perfume like. Beautifully effective in relieving constipation, green cardamom will also help to control blood pressure.

FENNEL SEEDS

Have a distinctive taste which comes from the anise-liquorice family. Delivers a warm and sweet flavour. Fennel is commonly used to treat anaemia, help with digestion and reduce cholesterol.

BLACK CARDAMOM

The Queen of Spices, with a smoky and peppermint undertone. It is dried over hot coals, hence the smoky flavour. It is still used as a toothpaste in rural parts of India and is a source of potassium, calcium and magnesium.

CLOVES

A spice which adds real depth and complexity of flavour, but should be used sparingly. Cloves help with digestion, have anti-microbial properties, protect the liver, boost the immune system, preserve bone quality and control diabetes.

FENUGREEK LEAVES

Sweet, nutty flavours. I love using them in curries with potatoes and root vegetables. Fenugreek can alleviate digestive problems and cholesterol levels.

MANGO POWDER

A souring agent and also a great tenderiser for meats. It is made by drying out raw green mango skins and grinding them to a powder. As well as possessing an incredible flavor, they contain a range of vitamins, minerals and antioxidants.

KASHMIRI CHILLIES

These are the best chillies to use when you first start to experiment with Indian dishes. Kashmiri chillies are high in Vitamin C and quality antioxidants so amazing for glowing skin.'

BREAKFAST STARTERS & SIDE DISHES

I have a very close relationship with my mother-in-law. This antique teapot and milk jug belong to her. I love listening to Norma's stories and going through the beautiful artefacts which she has kept safe for a lifetime.

Dad's Anti-Ageing Breakfast

Preparation time 30 minutes,
cooking time 40 minutes

SERVES **2**

KEY SPICES
1 tsp cumin seeds
¼ tsp black peppercorns

¼ tsp turmeric powder
1 tsp red chilli flakes

OTHER SPICES
2 tsp mango powder
¼ tsp dry ginger powder

WET INGREDIENTS
2 tbs sprouted mung beans
½ grapefruit, segmented
1 large orange, segmented
8 watermelon balls
8 papaya balls
2 fresh figs, quartered
2 dates, chopped
1 banana, sliced
10 raspberries
10 strawberries
10 seedless grapes, halved
2 tbs fresh pomegranate seeds

3 tbs low fat yogurt
2 tbs runny honey
Juice and zest of one lime

Pinch of sea salt

Place the cumin seeds and black peppercorns in a dry frying pan over a low heat and warm through for 1 minute.

Remove from the heat and grind in a pestle and mortar. Set aside.

Place all the wet ingredients in a large bowl. Sprinkle over the turmeric powder, red chilli flakes, mango powder, dry ginger powder and the contents of the pestle and mortar.

Stir and coat the wet ingredients really well.

Mix the yogurt, honey, lime juice and zest together, add to the bowl, and mix well.

Place the bowl in the fridge for 30 minutes, this dish is best served chilled especially in the summer.

Remove from the fridge, add a pinch of sea salt, stir well and serve cold.

Growing up Dad would make this breakfast outdoors in the early morning during the summer months. At this time of year he preferred this breakfast to aloo paratha, which was usually made in the winter months. Our neighbour Pat used to say that she could feel it doing her good whilst she ate it.

Stir-Fried Asparagus with a hint of Ginger, Lime and Cumin

Preparation time 20 minutes, cooking time 10-12 minutes

SERVES 4

450 g asparagus, washed, trimmed and dried with some kitchen paper.

KEY SPICES
½ tsp cumin seeds
¼ tsp black peppercorns
Pinch of red chilli flakes

WET INGREDIENTS
1 tbs groundnut oil
4 spring onions, chopped finely
1 tsp pulped ginger
2 tbs lime juice
Zest of one lime

½ tsp grated jaggery
Sea salt to taste
Handful of fresh coriander, chopped finely

Take a small dry frying pan set on a low heat, add the key spices and gently warm through for 1 minute - remember you just want to tease the spices to release a little of their oils, and rest of their flavours need to be retained to be infused into the asparagus.

Remove from the heat, place in a pestle and mortar, and grind to a powder. Set aside.

Heat a wok on a medium to high heat. One of the keys to successful stir-frying is pre-heating the wok before adding the oil, which should only take 1 minute. The wok should be just starting to smoke slightly. Add the oil which will heat up really quickly, then add the spring onions and ginger. Stir vigorously with a wooden spoon.

Add the contents of the pestle and mortar along with jaggery and sea salt to taste, stirring all the time. Add the asparagus and ensure it is coated well with the other ingredients.

You should then only need 1-2 minutes to stir-fry the asparagus.

Remove from the heat, add the lime juice, lime zest and fresh coriander.

Serve immediately.

The best tip for trimming is by bending the asparagus spear, it snaps at exactly the spot where the tough stalk meets the tender spear.

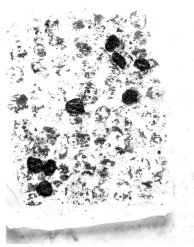

Easy Beetroot
& Pomegranate Crisps

Preparation time 10 minutes,
cooking time 25 minutes

SERVES 4

6 large uncooked beetroots

KEY SPICES
1 tsp cumin seeds

WARMING SPICES
1 tsp fennel seeds

OTHER SPICES
1 tbs pomegranate powder

WET INGREDIENTS
2 tbs coconut oil
1 tsp pulped ginger

Sea salt to taste

Preheat the oven to 375 F / 190 C / gas mark 5.

Place the cumin seeds and fennel seeds in a small frying pan and dry roast on a low heat until fragrant. Place in a pestle and mortar, grind to a fine powder. Set aside.

Peel the beetroot. Using a mandolin, slice thinly to 1.5 mm.

Once sliced, place in a bowl and drizzle with the oil, pomegranate powder, sea salt, add the pulped ginger as well as the fennel and cumin from the pestle and mortar. Stir well with your hands

Line a baking tray with grease-proof paper, and place the sliced beetroot in the tray.

Bake for 10-15 minutes. Remove from the oven, turn the crisps over, and bake for a further 5 minutes.

Tamarind, Carrot & Cumin Muffins

Preparation time 20 minutes, cooking time 50 minutes

SERVES 4

KEY SPICES
2 tsp cumin seeds
1 tsp red chilli flakes
1/4 tsp black peppercorns

WARMING SPICES
1 tsp fenugreek leaves
2 cloves

WET INGREDIENTS
1 tbs rapeseed oil
1 large onion, sliced thinly
1 tsp pulped garlic
150 g carrot, grated
80 g unsalted butter, melted
2 medium sized eggs
3 tbs tamarind pulp
275 g natural whole milk yogurt
2 tbs fresh coriander, chopped finely

OTHER INGREDIENTS
250 g plain flour
1 tsp baking powder
½ tsp bicarbonate of soda
12 muffin paper cases
1 tsp caster sugar
40 g pistachios, roughly crushed

Sea salt to taste

Pre-heat the oven to 200 C, 400 F or gas mark 6 and prepare the muffin tin with 12 paper cases.

Place a small dry frying pan on a low heat, then add the key spices and warming spices. Warm very gently for 1 minute.

Remove from the heat, place in a pestle and mortar, grind to a powder and set aside.

Place a medium sized sauté pan on a low heat, add the oil and allow it to warm, then add the onions with a pinch of sea salt and gently brown for 5 minutes.

Add the garlic, and the ground spices and continue to cook for a further 3 minutes.

Remove from the heat, stir in the grated carrot and allow to cool.

In a large bowl, sieve together the flour, baking powder, bicarbonate of soda, caster sugar and a pinch of sea salt.

In a separate bowl, whisk together the melted butter, eggs, tamarind, and yoghurt.

Add the contents of the two bowls together, then add the contents of the sauté pan and the fresh coriander.

Fold the ingredients with a spatula until thoroughly combined.

Spoon the mixture into the muffin cases and top with the pistachios.

Bake for about 18-20 minutes.

You can check if the muffins are cooked by placing a BBQ skewer in the middle of the muffin. If it comes out clear then the muffins are cooked.

This was a recipe originally created by accident. One of my Dad's friends asked him to bake some pakoras. They definitely tasted like pakoras, but looked more like muffins. I love cooking with tamarind, which has an incredible tangy and zesty flavour.

Carrots Stuffed with Pistachios and Coconut

Preparation time 30 minutes, cooking time 60 minutes

SERVES 2

4 large carrots, trimmed, cleaned, washed and cut twice to reduce to 3 equal lengths
50 g roasted pistachios, roughly ground
50 g fresh coconut

KEY SPICES
1 tsp cumin seeds
1 tsp brown mustard seeds

½ tsp turmeric powder
1 tsp red chilli flakes

WARMING SPICES
¼ tsp nigella seeds
1 tsp fennel seeds
1 tsp fenugreek leaves

OTHER SPICES
¼ tsp ajwain seeds

WET INGREDIENTS
2 tbs coconut oil
1 onion, chopped finely
1 tsp sundried tomato paste
2 tsp pulped garlic
1 tsp pulped ginger
2 fresh green chillies, minced (you can remove seeds and membrane for a milder dish, although carrots are rather sweet. Generally they benefit from keeping the membrane intact)
1 tbs pomegranate molasses
Zest and juice of one small lime
¼ pint of good hot vegetable stock

Sea salt to taste
1 tsp grated jaggery
Small bunch of fresh coriander, chopped finely including the stalks

GARNISH
Small bunch of fresh mint, finely chopped

Place the carrots in a saucepan of water and boil for at least 10 minutes. Remove from the heat, drain and cool the carrots under a cold tap to stop the cooking process.

Carefully remove the centre of the carrots with an apple corer. Set aside.
In a small dry frying pan, add the cumin seeds, mustard seeds, warming spices and ajwain seeds and gently warm for 1 minute.

Remove from the heat, place in a pestle and mortar and grind to a powder. Set aside.

Place a large sauté pan on a low heat, add the coconut oil and allow to warm.

Add the onion and salt to taste, and sauté for about 5 minutes, until a light golden-brown colour.

Add the turmeric powder, red chilli flakes, and sundried tomato paste, and continue to sauté for 5 minutes.

Add the garlic, ginger, chillies, jaggery and the contents of the pestle and mortar, and continue to cook for 10 minutes. If the mixture starts to become dry, add a little water.

Add the coconut, stir really well and cook for 1 minute.

Add the pomegranate molasses and pistachios. Stir really well, then immediately remove from the heat.

Add the lime zest, lime juice and fresh coriander.

Leave to cool and then carefully fill each carrot with the mixture from the sauté pan.

Place the carrots in an ovenproof dish, pour over the hot vegetable stock and bake in the oven for 10 minutes on 200°C / 390°F or gas mark 6.

Remove from the oven, sprinkle over the fresh mint and serve immediately.

This recipe originated one year when the carrots in our back garden were especially large. The filling of coconut and pistachios is a wonderful combination. Our neighbours, Mr and Mrs Mayo, raved about this dish for months afterwards.

Spicy Courgette Tempura Fries with Chickpea Flour

Preparation time 20 minutes,
cooking time 20 minutes

SERVES **4**

6 large courgettes (zucchini), washed, dried
and cut into thick matchsticks
150 g chickpea flour

KEY SPICES
1 tsp cumin seeds
½ tsp turmeric powder
1 tsp red chilli flakes

WARMING SPICES
1 tsp fenugreek leaves, soaked in 2 tbs of
hot water

OTHER SPICES
¼ tsp ajwain seeds
2 tsp mango powder

Sea salt to taste

WET INGREDIENTS
1 large egg, whisked
100 ml sparkling water
1 tsp pulped garlic
2 tsp pulped ginger
2 green chillies, minced
1 tsp rice wine vinegar
1 tsp baking powder

Vegetable oil for deep frying

Small bunch of fresh coriander, chopped
roughly

Place the cumin seeds and ajwain seeds in a small dry frying pan on a low heat, and warm through for 1 minute. Remove from the heat, place in a pestle and mortar and grind coarsely. Set aside.

Sieve the chickpea flour into a large bowl, then add the turmeric powder, red chilli flakes, fenugreek leaves, whisked egg, sparkling water, garlic, ginger, green chillies, rice wine vinegar, sea salt to taste and the contents of the pestle and mortar.

Whisk to make a smooth batter, add the mango powder and baking powder, and whisk really well.

Add the coriander and the courgettes, and cover with the batter.

Heat the oil in a large deep frying pan and carefully place large spoonfuls of the batter mixture into the hot oil.

Fry in batches for 2-3 minutes, turn and fry for a further 2 minutes, or until they are golden-brown.

Carefully remove from the oil and drain on kitchen paper.

Serve immediately. I like to eat this dish with peach and roasted shallot chutney (see page 184)

When I was young, we grew courgettes in our back garden. We used to sit outdoors with neighbours and friends while Dad and our neighbour, Mr Mayo, fried the courgettes and served them in brown paper bags which Dad used to save from our trips to the greengrocer.

Courgette and Red Onion Pakoras

Preparation time 60 minutes,
cooking time 20 minutes

SERVES 4

3 medium size courgettes (zucchinis)
1 large red onion, finely sliced

KEY SPICES
1 tsp cumin seeds
1 tsp coriander seeds

1 tsp red chilli flakes

WARMING SPICES
2 tsp fenugreek leaves

OTHER SPICES
1/2 tsp ajwain seeds
2 tsp mango powder

WET INGREDIENTS
1 tsp pulped garlic
1/2 tsp pulped ginger
2 fresh green chillies, finely minced (I leave
the seeds and membrane in, but feel free
to remove both if you want to make milder
pakoras)
Juice of half a lime
A little extra water if required
Vegetable oil for deep frying

1 small bunch coriander including the
stalks, chopped roughly
1/2 tsp baking soda
Sea salt to sprinkle and taste

Grate the courgettes into a large bowl, add the sliced red onion and sprinkle a little sea salt over them.

Stir well and leave for about 60 minutes.

Drain and rinse the courgettes well, squeeze out the excess water, then place in a large bowl.

Place a small dry pan on a low heat, and warm through the cumin seeds, coriander seeds, fenugreek leaves and ajwain seeds for 1 minute.

Remove from the heat, place in a pestle and mortar, and grind to a fine powder.

Add the contents of the pestle and mortar, red chilli flakes and mango powder to the large bowl. Stir really well.

Add garlic, ginger, green chillies, lime juice, fresh coriander, baking soda and salt to taste.

The best way to mix this really well is using your hands, but feel free to use a spatula to produce a thick batter. Add a splash of water to loosen the batter if it feels too stiff.

Heat the oil in a deep pot to 350 F or 180 C. Carefully place small balls of the courgette-onion batter into the hot oil.

Fry and turn often for 3 - 4 minutes, or until the pakoras are golden-brown and crispy.

Carefully remove the pakoras from the oil, using a slotted spoon, and drain well on kitchen paper.

Serve hot with your favourite chutneys.

This was my Dad's ultimate garden party-piece. He would literally fry these all night in his makeshift fire, for all the kids playing in the garden.

Potatoes Cooked in Mint & Tamarind

Preparation time 20 minutes, cooking time 25 minutes

SERVES 4

750 g potatoes, peeled and cut into 1 inch cubes (I love using Maris Piper potatoes for this dish)

KEY SPICES
½ tsp turmeric powder
½ tsp brown mustard seeds
1 tsp cumin seeds
1 tsp red chilli flakes
1 Indian bay leaf

WARMING SPICES
1 tsp fennel seeds
¼ tsp nigella seeds
1 tsp fenugreek leaves, soaked in 2 tbs of hot water

OTHER SPICES
½ tsp asafoetida
½ tsp ajwain seeds
1 tsp mango powder
1 tsp dry mint leaves

WET INGREDIENTS
3 tbs groundnut oil or vegetable oil
1 heaped tsp tomato paste
1 tsp pulped garlic
1 tsp pulped ginger
2 tbs pulped tamarind

Rock salt or salt flakes to taste
2 tbs natural yogurt
Small bunch of fresh coriander, roughly chopped

Parboil the potatoes in a large pan with a pinch of salt and the turmeric, this usually takes about 5 minutes.

Drain in a colander and place a kitchen towel over the top of the colander, so that the potatoes steam dry. Set aside.

Place a large sauté pan on a low heat and add the oil. Once the oil is warm, add the mustard seeds, fennel seeds, nigella seeds, asafoetida and ajwain seeds. Stir well into the oil, then stir in all of the remaining key spices, and fry until fragrant.

Add the tomato paste, garlic and ginger. Stir and fry for 1 minute.

Add the potatoes, coat and stir really well. Ensure that the potatoes are cooked through, and a little crispy on the outside.

Add the fenugreek leaves, mango powder, mint leaves, and tamarind pulp.

Cook for a further minute, remove from the heat, place a lid on the pan and leave for 10 minutes.

Add fresh coriander, and serve with chapattis and a little natural yogurt

After eating this dish, someone once said to me 'Who would have thought that potatoes could taste so good?' Mint has an incredibly distinctive flavour and it is also very good at promoting digestion. With incredible tamarind pulp playing a key role in this dish too, it will definitely impress any foodie.

Masala Potatoes

Preparation time 20 minutes,
cooking time 35 minutes

SERVES 4

KEY SPICES
1 tsp brown mustard seeds
1 tsp crushed coriander seeds
1 tsp cumin seeds
1 tsp red chilli flakes
1 1 inch piece of cassia bark

WARMING SPICES
1 tsp fennel seeds
1 tsp fenugreek leaves, soaked in 2 tbs hot water

OTHER INGREDIENTS
2 tsp asafoetida
1 tsp Himalayan pink rock salt
¼ tsp nigella seeds
1 tbs mango powder
5 tbs water

WET INGREDIENTS
4 medium size potatoes, cubed
3 tbs vegetable oil
1 tsp pulped garlic
1 tsp pulped ginger
2 medium size fresh tomatoes, chopped finely
6 fresh curry leaves, ripped
Small bunch of fresh coriander, coarsely chopped

Peel and wash the potatoes in cold water to get rid of any extra starch. Then cut into small cubes and place in a large pot. Cover with cold water, add 1 tsp asafoetida and the rock salt.

Bring to the boil and cook for about 5 minutes. Drain in a colander, cover with kitchen paper and leave to steam dry.

Add the vegetable oil to a large sauté pan and heat on a medium heat. Add 1 tsp of asafoetida and the key spices.

Reduce the heat to low, and stir well, until aromatic. This should take about one minute.

Add the warming spices, nigella seeds, mango powder, garlic, curry leaves and ginger, and cook for a further 2 minutes.

Add the fresh tomatoes and cook for a further 10 minutes on a low simmer with the lid on, stirring occasionally.

Add the potatoes, stir really well, and then add 5 tbs of water.

Reduce to a low simmer, place the lid on the pan and cook for 10 minutes.

Remove from the heat, and add the chopped coriander.

We had family and friends who would often arrive at our house unannounced. It was our custom to always feed them and this was a quick and easy recipe. As well as being a great natural source of many important vitamins and minerals, I have always found potatoes to be a wonderfully versatile ingredient to cook with.

Bombay Potato with Rhubarb

Preparation time 30 minutes, cooking time 55 minutes

SERVES FOUR

3 pink rhubarb stalks, cut into 1 inch chunks. Rhubarb leaves should be removed.
850 g large potatoes, peeled and cut into large chunks
1 tbs brown sugar

KEY SPICES
1 tsp cumin seeds
1 tsp crushed coriander seeds
1 tsp brown mustard seeds
½ tsp black peppercorns

1 1 inch piece of cassia bark
1 Indian bay leaf

1 and ½ tsp turmeric powder
1 tsp red chilli flakes

WARMING SPICES
½ tsp fennel seeds
1 tsp fenugreek leaves, soaked in 2tbs of hot water
½ tsp nigella seeds
2 cloves

WET INGREDIENTS
4 tbs groundnut oil or vegetable oil
1 large onion, finely chopped
2 large tomatoes, roughly chopped
2 tsp pulped garlic
1 tsp pulped ginger
2 green chillies, pierced
1 small bunch of coriander including stalks, roughly chopped

1 tsp rock salt or salt flakes
1 tsp grated jaggery

Pre heat the oven to gas mark 4, 350°F (180°C).

Place the rhubarb stalks on a non-stick baking try and sprinkle the brown sugar over the top. Bake in a pre-heated oven for 10 minutes. Remove and set aside.

Place a large saucepan of water on the boil, with 1 tsp of turmeric powder and 1 tsp of salt. Parboil the potatoes for 7 minutes.

Drain the potatoes in a colander, and place a kitchen towel over the top (this will steam dry the potatoes). Set aside.

Take a small dry frying pan, set on a low heat, and warm through the cumin seeds, coriander seeds, brown mustard seeds and black peppercorns until fragrant. This should take 1 minute, as you are just trying to tease the oil out of the spices. Remove from the heat, add to the pestle and mortar and grind coarsely.

Take a large sauté pan, add the oil and warm on a low heat. Then add the onions, cassia bark, Indian bay leaf and salt to taste. Sauté for 5 minutes.

Add the ½ tsp of turmeric and red chilli flakes, stir and sauté for 2 minutes.

Add the chopped tomatoes and jaggery, and continue to sauté for a further 10 minutes, stirring occasionally.

By cooking these ingredients for a little longer, your curry will definitely taste better.

Now add the garlic, ginger and green chillies, and sauté for 2 minutes.

Add the contents of the pestle and mortar, stir well, and sauté for about 10 minutes, until you see that the mixture resembles a paste.

If the paste becomes a little dry and sticks to the pan, then just add a little water whenever you need, to help you achieve the required consistency.

Add the parboiled potatoes and baked rhubarb, and stir really well on a high heat for 1 minute.

Now take the frying pan again, and on a low heat warm the fennel seeds, nigella seeds and cloves for 1 minute. Remove from the heat and grind coarsely.

Reduce the heat to simmer, add the warming spices including the fenugreek, place the lid on the pan, and cook for 10 minutes or until the potatoes are cooked through.

Remove from the heat, add the chopped coriander including the stalks.
Serve with a roasted almond and coriander chutney (see page 187) and warm chapattis.

This was one of my childhood favourite dishes. My Dad used to love making this, with rhubarb picked fresh from our back garden.

Punjabi Aloo Gobi

Preparation time 20 minutes, cooking time 40 minutes

SERVES: 4

2 small cauliflowers, separated into small florets
2 large potatoes, peeled and cut into large chunks

KEY SPICES
1 tsp cumin seeds
1 tsp coriander seeds

1 1 inch piece of cassia bark
1 Indian bay leaf

¼ tsp turmeric powder
1 tsp red chilli flakes

WARMING SPICES
2 tsp fenugreek leaves, soaked in 4tbs hot water

OTHER SPICES
¼ tsp asafoetida
2 tsp mango powder

WET INGREDIENTS
3 tbs vegetable oil
2 medium onions, chopped finely
2 large fresh tomatoes, chopped finely
1 tsp pulped garlic
2 tsp pulped ginger
2 green chillies, pierced

Sea salt to taste

GARNISH
Small bunch of fresh coriander including the stalks, chopped roughly
Juice and zest of 1 small lime

Heat a small frying pan on a low heat, add the cumin seeds and coriander seeds, and warm for 1 minute. Remove from the heat, add to a pestle and mortar and grind coarsely. Set aside.

Place a large sauté pan on a low heat, add the oil and asafoetida. Once the oil is warm, add the onions and sauté for 5 minutes.

Add the cassia bark, bay leaf and sea salt to taste. Continue to sauté for a further 5 minutes.

Add the turmeric powder and red chilli flakes, and continue to sauté for 2 minutes.

Add the tomatoes, garlic, ginger, green chillies, and the contents of the pestle and mortar.

Sauté for about 10 minutes until the mixture looks like a paste. If the mixture becomes dry, just add a little water.

Add the potatoes, stir and coat well. Sauté for 5 minutes on a medium heat, adding a little water to help cook the potatoes.

Add the cauliflower florets, stir and coat well. Sauté for 2 -3 minutes.

Add the fenugreek leaves and mango powder. Reduce to a simmer, cover with the lid and cook until the potatoes and cauliflower are tender.

Remove from the heat, add the coriander including the stalks, as well as the lime juice and zest.

Stir well and serve with chapattis

We used to grow cauliflowers in our back garden. This was a dish we loved, and which my Dad would quickly make for unexpected guests. Anyone that came to our house never left without eating something. That included the postman, milkman, rag and bone man, and even the old man who delivered paraffin and coal to our house.

Spicy Tomatoes with Eggs

Preparation time 15 minutes,
cooking time 20 minutes

SERVES 4

4 large beef tomatoes, tops cut and seeds
removed to create a hallow space
4 small free range eggs

KEY SPICES
1 tsp cumin seeds
½ tsp black peppercorns
1 tsp red chilli flakes

WARMING SPICES
1 tsp fenugreek leaves

WET INGREDIENTS
1 tbs softened unsalted butter
½ tsp pulped garlic
½ tsp pulped ginger
1 tbs fresh coriander stalks, chopped

GARNISH
Small bunch of fresh coriander, finely
chopped
Fresh mild red chilli, finely minced

Sea salt to taste

Preheat the oven to 200 C, 390 F or gas mark 6.

Place the tomatoes on a baking sheet, slice a little off the bottom of each tomato so that they sit flat on the baking sheet.

Place a small dry frying pan on a low heat, add the key spices and warming spices, and warm for 1 minute.

Remove from the heat, transfer to a pestle and mortar and grind to a powder.

Transfer the contents of the pestle and mortar to a bowl. Add the softened butter, garlic, ginger, coriander stalks and salt to taste. Mix really well.

Take each tomato, and using a pastry brush, coat the inside really well with the mixture from the bowl.

Crack one egg into each tomato. Season with a little sea salt.

Place in the oven for 8 - 10 minutes, or if you like the eggs runny for 6 - 7 minutes.

Remove from the oven and garnish with fresh chopped coriander and red chilli.

Serve with your favourite toast.

A quick and easy breakfast, which is ideal if you have guests staying.

Spinach and Onion Pakoras

Preparation time 20 minutes, cooking time 20 minutes. Overnight refrigeration required.

SERVES 4

3 sliced large potatoes (King Edwards are my favourites for making pakoras)
2 large onions, finely sliced
220 g of baby spinach
Small bunch of fresh coriander, chopped
150-200 g chickpea flour

KEY SPICES
½ tsp turmeric powder
1 tsp red chilli flakes

1 tsp cumin seeds
¼ tsp crushed black peppercorns
½ tsp crushed coriander seeds

WARMING SPICES
2 tsp fenugreek leaves, soaked in 4 tbs of hot water for 10 minutes

OTHER SPICES
1 tsp ajwain
1 tsp pomegranate powder
1 tsp mango powder

WET INGREDIENTS
1 tbs fresh lemon juice
Vegetable oil, for deep frying

Rock salt or salt flakes

Slice the potatoes and onions thinly into a large mixing bowl. Add the baby spinach, coriander, turmeric powder, red chilli flakes, soaked fenugreek leaves and lemon juice. Sprinkle salt over, and leave in the fridge overnight.

NB: I place a small side plate on top of the ingredients in the mixing bowl with a heavy object on top of the plate to help draw the water from the fresh ingredients. My heavy object is my pestle and mortar.

Remove from the fridge and you will find that the salt (and your weighted object) has drawn all the water out of the ingredients.

In a dry pan, roast the remaining key spices, and other spices, until fragrant.

Add all of the roasted spices from the dry pan to the mixing bowl and stir in.

Gradually add gram flour to the mixing bowl, until the mixture is the consistency of pancake batter but not quite as runny.

Over a medium-high heat in a large, heavy saucepan, heat the oil to 375° C or 190 F.

Carefully place spoonfuls of the pakora mixture into the oil.

Once the potato slices are golden in colour, carefully take the pakoras out of the oil, and put them on some kitchen paper to absorb any excess oil.

Serve hot with fiery mint chutney (see page 177) and masala chai.

If you find that the wet ingredients have not released enough natural water, add a little extra water, sufficient to make the batter. Only add this if you have to, and be careful not to add too much.

I hope you really like the method for this recipe. Many versions of the dish have added water helping to create the batter. My recipe uses the natural juices from the onions and spinach instead. You will create a much tastier and lighter paokra using this recipe.

QUICK
& SALAD RECIPES

My Dad's tiffin tin is over 60 years old. He used to work shifts at a rubber factory and took food to work in this tiffin tin. He started a supper club for the nightshift, which was so typical of him, using his amazing food to bring people together.

Carrot, cashew and sultana salad with cumin seeds

Preparation time 20 minutes, cooking time 10 minutes

SERVES 4

4 medium size carrots, washed, peeled and cut into thin strips (using a potato peeler)

KEY SPICES
1 tsp cumin seeds

OTHER INGREDIENTS
1 tbs groundnut oil
½ tsp pulped ginger
1 tbs white wine vinegar
1 tbs brown sugar
2 tbs honey
25 g sultanas, soaked in 5 tbs of hot orange juice
25 g roasted cashews
2 tbs fresh coriander leaves, finely chopped
Sea salt to taste

Blanch the carrots in hot water for 1 minute, drain and run under cold water to stop the cooking process. Then place on absorbent kitchen paper and set aside.

Place a dry frying pan on a low heat, add the groundnut oil, allow to warm, add the cumin seeds and allow them to brown very slightly.

Add the ginger and sauté for 30 seconds.

Add the white wine vinegar and sauté for 30 seconds.

Add the brown sugar, honey and sultanas soaked in orange juice, and simmer until you have a sticky consistency.

Remove from the heat and set aside.

Roughly crush the cashew nuts, add to a large bowl along with the carrots, then pour over the dressing from the frying pan and add the coriander.

Toss the salad really well, and season with sea salt just before serving.

Gujarati Carrot Salad

Preparation time 20 minutes.
Cooking time 2-3 minutes.

SERVES 4

200g carrots, coarsely grated
100 g pomegranate seeds

KEY SPICES
1 tsp cumin seeds
¼ tsp red chilli flakes

WARMING SPICES
¼ tsp fennel seeds
¼ tsp nigella seeds
¼ tsp fenugreek leaves

WET INGREDIENTS
1 tbs groundnut oil
3 tbs fresh lemon juice
1 tbs clear honey
6 curry leaves chopped finely (optional)

Sea salt to taste
Handful of fresh coriander leaves, roughly chopped

Place the carrots and pomegranate seeds into a large bowl. Set aside.

Heat the oil in a pan over a low heat, add the key spices, warming spices and sea salt to taste. Sauté for 1 minute until fragrant.

Add the lemon juice, honey and curry leaves. Warm through, then allow to cool.

Add to the bowl of carrots and pomegranate, along with the fresh coriander. Stir well.

Serve immediately.

In the summer we used to take these salads to the local park and eat them wrapped in fresh chapattis. I have always loved cooking with pomegranates which have an incredible ruby colour and are high in antioxidants. Each pomegranate contains hundreds of small crisp arils, each encased in moist pulp.

Tangy tamarind, carrot and red cabbage salad

Preparation time 20 minutes, cooking time 20 minutes

SERVES 4

4 large carrots, grated
1 small red cabbage, grated

KEY SPICES
1 tsp cumin seeds

½ tsp turmeric powder
1 tsp red chilli flakes

WARMING SPICES
1 tsp fennel seeds
1 tsp fenugreek leaves
½ tsp nigella seeds

WET INGREDIENTS
1 tbs groundnut oil
1 large red onion, finely sliced
1 tsp pulped garlic
½ tsp pulped ginger
1 mild red chilli, pierced
1 tbs white wine vinegar
1 tbs tamarind pulp

1 tbs grated jaggery

GARNISH
Zest of one lime
Juice of one lime
25 g roasted cashew nuts, roughly chopped
1 small bunch of coriander including stalks, roughly chopped
1 small bunch of mint leaves, roughly chopped

Place a dry frying pan on a low heat, place the cumin seeds and the warming spices in the pan, and gently warm through for 1 minute. Remove from the heat, add to the pestle and mortar and grind to a powder. Set aside.

In a large sauté pan add the oil and add warm through on a medium to low heat.

Add the red onion and sauté for 2 minutes.

Add the spices from the pestle and mortar, as well as the turmeric powder, red chilli flakes, garlic, ginger, mild red chilli, white wine vinegar and jaggery, and continue to sauté for a further 5 minutes or until the onions are golden-brown.

Add the tamarind pulp, stir well and immediately remove from the heat.

Add in the carrots and red cabbage, stir well and allow to sit for 5 minutes.

Add in the lime zest, lime juice, cashew nuts, coriander and mint. Toss the salad really well and serve.

This salad goes really well with grilled meats. 'Sometimes simplicity is best' my Dad used to say. Just let the flavour do the talking.

Indian Warm Potato Salad

Preparation time 20 minutes,
cooking time 30 minutes

SERVES 4

700 g Charlotte or Anya potatoes
1 large red pepper, deseeded and
cut into strips
1 large green pepper, deseeded and cut
into strips

KEY SPICES
1 tsp cumin seeds
1 tsp brown mustard seeds
2 tsp red chilli flakes
½ tsp turmeric powder

WARMING SPICES
1 tsp fennel seeds
1 tsp fenugreek leaves
¼ tsp nigella seeds

OTHER SPICES
½ tsp asafoetida
2 tsp mango powder

WET INGREDIENTS
2 tbs rapeseed oil
2 tsp pulped garlic
1 tsp pulped ginger
2 - 3 fresh whole green chillies, pierced
5 tbs sour cream

1 tsp grated jaggery
Sea salt to taste

GARNISH
Small bunch of fresh coriander, chopped
Zest and juice of one lime

Steam the potatoes in a steamer or over a pan of simmering water for 10 minutes, with ½ tsp of asafoetida and a pinch of sea salt added to the water.

Remove the potatoes from the water and allow to cool. Once cool slice the potatoes into half lengthways and set aside.

Place a small dry frying pan on a low heat, add all the key spices and warming spices to the pan and warm through for 1 minute.

Remove from the heat, add to a pestle and mortar grind to a powder and set aside.

Take a large sauté pan set on a low heat, add the oil and once warm add the ground spices. Stir and allow them to sizzle for just 30 seconds.

Add the garlic, ginger, chillies and jaggery, and sauté for 1 minute. You can add a splash of water if the spices begin to stick to the pan.

Add the red and green peppers and mango powder, stir really well and sauté for 1 minute.

Add the potatoes and sea salt to taste. Stir and cook for 2 minutes.

Add the sour cream, stirring really well, and cook for 2 minutes.

Remove from the heat, add the fresh coriander, lime juice and zest, stir and serve warm.

I created this one day, on reflecting that too many potato salads contain mayonnaise. Potatoes are an ingredient which always retain and promote the flavours of spices really well.

Cooked Cucumber with Coconut

Preparation time 20 minutes, cooking time 20 minutes

SERVES 4

2 large fresh cucumbers
60 g freshly grated coconut (frozen is fine)

KEY SPICES
½ tsp turmeric powder
1 tsp red chilli flakes

1 tsp cumin seeds
1 tsp brown mustard seeds

WARMING SPICES
1 tsp fennel seeds
1 tsp fenugreek leaves
¼ tsp nigella seeds

WET INGREDIENTS
2 tbs coconut oil
6-8 curry leaves, ripped
1 tsp pulped garlic
1 tsp pulped ginger
1 fresh mild red chilli, chopped finely (you can remove the seeds and membrane if you want a really mild flavouring, but I think the cucumber really works with a little heat)
1 tbs tamarind pulp
Juice of half a lime
Zest of a lime
Small bunch of fresh coriander, roughly chopped

Cut the cucumbers lengthways, and scoop out the flesh with a teaspoon.

Dice the cucumber, and place on some kitchen paper to absorb most of the water. Set aside.

In a small dry frying pan, warm the cumin seeds, mustard seeds and warming spices for 1 minute on a low heat.

Remove from the pan, place in pestle and mortar, and grind to a powder. Set aside.

In the same pan, gently roast the grated coconut.

Be vigilant while you are doing this, or the coconut will burn. Stir continuously for light golden-brown grated coconut.

Remove the coconut from the heat, place in a bowl and add the contents of the pestle and mortar, turmeric powder and red chilli flakes. Mix together well and set aside.

Heat the coconut oil in a medium size sauté pan on a low heat.

Add the curry leaves, garlic, ginger and mild red chilli, and sauté for 1 minute.

Add the contents of the bowl to the sauté pan. Stir and sauté for 1 minute.

Add the tamarind pulp and cucumber, then cook for 5-7 minutes, stirring really well.

Remove from the heat, add the lime juice, lime zest and fresh coriander.

My Dad and I first made this dish when he came home with a box of cucumbers from our local greengrocers. He had been given them, along with an assortment of many other vegetables, in exchange for helping the greengrocer to change the spark plugs on his van. This is a great dish to serve outdoors, either hot or cold, on a warm summer evening.

Spicy Warm Roasted Tomato and Cumin Salad

Preparation time 15 minutes, cooking time 25 minutes

SERVES 4

20 cherry tomatoes

KEY SPICES
1 tsp cumin seeds
1 tsp coriander seeds
1 tsp red chilli flakes
1/4 tsp black peppercorns

WARMING SPICES
1 tsp fennel seeds

OTHER SPICES
Pinch of asafoetida
1 tsp mango powder

WET INGREDIENTS
2 tbs vegetable oil
1 medium sized onion, diced finely
2 tsp pulped garlic
1 tsp pulped ginger
1 tbs white wine vinegar

Sea salt to taste
1 tsp grated jaggery
Small bunch of coriander, chopped

Place a small dry frying pan on a low heat, add the key spices and fennel seeds, and warm for 1 minute.

Remove from the heat, place in a pestle and mortar, grind to a powder and set aside.

Heat the oil in a sauté pan on a medium heat, add the asafoetida and allow to sizzle, then immediately add the onion and salt, and sauté until golden-brown for about 5 minutes.

Add the garlic, ginger, white wine vinegar, jaggery, the contents of the pestle and mortar and mango powder, then sauté on a low heat for 5 minutes.

Stir in the cherry tomatoes and turn the heat to a high simmer, cook the tomatoes until they start to blister. Remove from the heat, add the fresh coriander and serve.

This salad is humble yet amazing. It looks great on the plate and I love the flavour combination of tomato and cumin. Cumin is one of my very favourite spices, and is a great natural remedy for digestive problems as well as boosting the immune system.

Quick Stir-Fried Asparagus with Coconut

Preparation time 20 minutes, cooking time 10 minutes

SERVES 4

30 asparagus spears, washed, trimmed and dried with some kitchen paper. The best tip for trimming is by bending the asparagus spear, it snaps at exactly the spot where the tough stalk meets the tender spear.
50 g freshly grated coconut (frozen is fine)

KEY SPICES
1 tsp cumin seeds
1 tsp brown mustard seeds
1 tsp red chilli flakes

WARMING SPICES
1 tsp fennel seeds
1 tsp fenugreek seeds
¼ tsp nigella seeds

WET INGREDIENTS
1.5 tbs pure virgin coconut oil
8 fresh curry leaves, ripped (optional)
1 tsp pulped garlic
2 tsp pulped ginger
2 - 3 red or green chillies, pierced
Juice and zest of one small lime

Sea salt to taste
Small bunch of fresh coriander chopped including stalks

Heat the wok on a medium heat for 30 seconds, then add the oil, key spices, warming spices and curry leaves. Heat through for 1 minute.

Stirring continuously add the garlic, ginger and chillies.

Add the asparagus and toss to ensure that it is well coated with the other ingredients.

Cook on a high heat for about 2 to 3 minutes.

Add the grated coconut and toss well to ensure that the coconut is well distributed.

Add sea salt to taste and remove from the heat.

Add the lime juice, lime zest and fresh coriander, then serve.

This is a great side, which goes really well with a lamb or even a fish dish.

Quick Beetroot Curry

Preparation time 10 minutes,
cooking time 15 minutes

SERVES 4

600g cooked beetroot, chopped into
bitesize pieces

KEY SPICES
1 tsp cumin seeds
½ tsp brown mustard seeds
1 tsp crushed coriander seeds (you can
crush the seeds in a pestle and mortar)
2 dry whole red chillies

WARMING SPICES
1 tsp fenugreek leaves
1 tsp fennel seeds

OTHER SPICES
2 tsp mango powder

WET INGREDIENTS
2 tbs coconut oil
2 tsp pulped garlic
1 tsp pulped ginger
140 ml water
140 ml coconut milk

6-8 curry leaves, snipped finely using
scissors
Sea salt to taste

GARNISH
Small bunch of fresh coriander, chopped
Juice and zest of one small lime

Heat the oil in a sauté pan on a low heat, then add the key spices, warming spices and curry leaves. Allow to warm for 1 minute.

Add the garlic, ginger, mango powder and sea salt to taste. Sauté for 2 minutes.

Add the water and coconut milk, bring to a boil, then immediately reduce to a simmer and add the beetroot.

Stir well, place the lid on the pan and sauté for about 7-8 minutes until most of the liquid has absorbed.

Remove from the heat and add the fresh coriander, lime juice and zest.

Serve with fresh chapattis.

My Dad always grew beetroot in our back garden, and I've been eating it since the age of four. I believe that it's one of the key reasons that I am wrinkle-free. Some people are reluctant to try this dish, but it tastes great and is really good for you. Beetroot is rich in immune-boosting vitamin C, fibre, and essential minerals like manganese and potassium.

Quick & Easy Carrot & Fenugreek

Preparation time 20 minutes
cooking time 20 minutes

SERVES 4

6 medium size carrots, sliced and blanched in hot water for 2 minutes

KEY SPICES
½ tsp turmeric powder
1 tsp red chilli flakes

1 tsp cumin seeds
1 tsp brown mustard seeds

WARMING SPICES
1 tsp fennel seeds
¼ tsp nigella seeds
1 heaped teaspoon fenugreek leaves, soaked in 2 tbs hot water

OTHER SPICES
¼ tsp ajwain seeds
1 tbs mango powder

WET INGREDIENTS
2 tbs vegetable oil
1 tsp pulped garlic
1 tsp pulped ginger
2 green chillies, pierced
1 medium sized tomato, chopped
2 tsp fresh lemon juice

Small bunch of fresh coriander, roughly chopped

Place the turmeric powder and red chilli flakes in a small bowl, add 1 tablespoon of hot water, stir and mix well. Set aside.

Place a small dry frying pan on a low heat. Add the cumin seeds, brown mustard seeds, fennel seeds, nigella seeds and ajwain seeds to the pan, and warm for 1 minute. Then place in the pestle and mortar, and grind coarsely. Set aside.

Take a large sauté pan, add the oil and warm through on a low heat.

Add the spices from the pestle and mortar, stir, add the garlic, ginger and pierced green chillies then sauté for 1-2 minutes.

Add the tomato and fry for 1 minute.

Add the carrots, stir well and coat.

Place a lid on the pan, and cook on a low heat for 10 minutes.

Add the soaked fenugreek leaves, mango powder and lemon juice. Cook for 3 minutes without the lid on. Remove from the heat, and add fresh coriander.

Enjoy with some natural yogurt and chapattis

This is a simple, fresh and flavoursome dish which you can create in very little time. I hope this healthy recipe will encourage you not to reach for the takeaway menu. Fenugreek is a wonderful tasting spice, which is good for digestive problems and is commonly used to help with diabetes and obesity.

Quick Chickpea with Eggs

Preparation time 15 minutes, cooking time 25 minutes

SERVES 4

400 g canned chickpeas, rinsed and drained
4 eggs, boiled and shelled

KEY SPICES
1 tsp cumin seeds
1 tsp brown mustard seeds
1 tsp red chilli flakes

WARMING SPICES
1 tsp fennel seeds
1 tsp fenugreek leaves
¼ tsp nigella seeds

OTHER SPICES
¼ tsp asafoetida
2 tsp mango powder

WET INGREDIENTS
2 tbs coconut oil
1 tsp pulped garlic
1 tsp pulped ginger
2 fresh green chillies, pierced
2 fresh medium size tomatoes, chopped roughly
1 tbs white wine vinegar
140 ml water

Sea salt to taste
Small bunch of fresh coriander, chopped

Place a sauté pan on a low heat, add the coconut oil and allow to warm, then add the asafoetida and allow to sizzle.

Immediately add the key spices and warming spices, stir and sauté for 1 minute.

Add the garlic, ginger, green chillies, tomatoes and white wine vinegar and sauté for 4 minutes.

Add the chickpeas, stir well and sauté for 1 minute.

Add the water, turn the heat to medium and sauté for 5 minutes, then reduce to a simmer and cook for a further 5 minutes with the lid on

Put a few slits in the eggs and add to the chickpeas. Sprinkle the mango powder over the mixture. Stir well, place the lid back on the pan and cook for 5 minutes.

Remove from the heat, add the fresh coriander and serve with chapattis.

This was a dish that Dad and I created one day when we realised that we had run out of potatoes. We boiled some eggs, added chickpeas and a blend of spices and it was an immediate favourite. Chickpeas are a good source of fibre and two to three tablespoons equate to one portion of the recommended five portions of fruit and vegetables per day.

Quick Paneer with Mango Pickle and Peppers

Preparation time 10 minutes, cooking time 15 minutes

SERVES 4

225 g paneer, chopped into bite size pieces
1 green pepper, cut into thin strips
1 red pepper, cut into thin strips

KEY SPICES
1 tsp cumin seeds
1 tsp brown mustard seeds
1 tsp red chilli flakes

WARMING SPICES
1 tsp fennel seeds
1 tsp fenugreek leaves
¼ tsp nigella seeds

OTHER SPICES
¼ tsp asafoetida

WET INGREDIENTS
2 tbs vegetable oil
1 tsp pulped garlic
1 tsp pulped ginger
2 fresh green chillies, pierced
1 medium fresh tomato, cut into thin wedges
2 tsp sundried tomato paste
2 tsp hot mango pickle, chopped finely
1 tbs lime juice

GARNISH
Small bunch of coriander, chopped
Zest of one small lime

Sea or rock salt

Place a sauté pan on a low heat, add the oil and allow to warm, then add asafoetida, stir and allow to sizzle.

Immediately add the key spices and warming spices and sauté for 2 minutes.

Add the garlic, ginger, green chillies, tomato, lime juice and sundried tomato paste. Stir well, add salt to taste and sauté for 2 minutes.

Add mango pickle, stir and sauté for a further 2 minutes.

Add the paneer, coat in all the spices by stirring well, and sauté on a medium heat for 2 minutes.

Add the peppers, stir well and cook for 1 minute.

Remove from the heat, place a lid on the pan and allow all the ingredients to infuse for 5 minutes.

Add fresh coriander and lime zest.

This is a great 'after work - no onion - quick fix curry'. A really easy dish which you can whip up in less than half an hour.

Quick Pepper Chicken Masala

Preparation time 30 minutes,
cooking time 60 minutes

SERVES 4-6

500 g mini chicken fillets, cut into large
cubes
1 green pepper, cut into thin strips
1 red pepper, cut into thin strips

KEY SPICES
1 tsp cumin seeds
1 tsp coriander seeds
1 tsp brown mustard seeds
¼ tsp crushed peppercorns

1 1 inch piece of cassia bark
1 Indian bay leaf

½ tsp turmeric powder
1 tsp red chilli flakes

WARMING SPICES
6 green cardamoms, lightly bashed
1 black cardamom, lightly bashed
1 tsp fennel seeds
3 dry whole Kashmiri chillies

1 tsp fenugreek seeds, soaked in 2 tbs hot
water

OTHER SPICES
½ tsp ajwain seeds

WET INGREDIENTS
1 tbs white wine vinegar
8 fresh curry leaves
3 tbs coconut oil
2 onions, finely chopped
3 medium size fresh tomatoes, puréed
2 tsp pulped garlic
2 tsp pulped ginger
2 fresh finger green chillies, pierced
140 ml water

1 tsp grated jaggery
Rock salt or salt flakes to taste
Small bunch of fresh coriander, roughly
chopped

Remove the chicken from the fridge, place in large bowl, add the white wine vinegar and allow the chicken to come to room temperature

Heat a small dry pan on a medium heat, and warm the green and black cardamoms, curry leaves, fennel seeds, whole red chillies and the ajwain seeds until fragrant. Remove from the heat and set aside.

Take a small dry frying pan, set on a low heat, and warm through the cumin seeds, coriander seeds, brown mustard seeds and black peppercorns until fragrant. This should take 1 minute, as you are just trying to tease the oil out of the spices. Remove from the heat, add to the pestle and mortar and grind coarsely.

Take a large sauté pan, add the oil and warm on a low heat. Then add the onions, cassia bark, Indian bay leaf and salt to taste. Sauté for 5 minutes.

Add the turmeric and red chilli flakes, stir and sauté for 2 minutes.

Add the chopped tomatoes and jaggery, and continue to sauté for a further 10 minutes, stirring occasionally.

By cooking these ingredients for a little longer, your curry will definitely taste better.

Now add the garlic, ginger and green chillies, and sauté for 2 minutes.

Add the contents of the pestle and mortar, stir well, and sauté for about 10 minutes, until you see that the mixture resembles a paste.

If the paste becomes a little dry and sticks to the pan, then just add a little water whenever you need, to help you achieve the required consistency.

Add all of the warming spices and curry leaves. Stir well and cook for 1 minute.

Add the chicken pieces, and stir well to coat them with the spices.

Add the water, bring to the boil, then reduce the heat to simmer, and cook with the lid on for about 15 minutes.

Stir occasionally, or until the chicken pieces are cooked through.

Add the green and red peppers, stir really well, then place the lid back on the pan, and switch off the heat. The steam should cook your peppers, leaving them slightly 'al dente'.

After 10 minutes lift the lid off the pan, and add the fresh coriander.

Serve with chapattis or cumin rice.

Remember to count your cardamoms in and count them out again before serving.

Quick and Easy Runner Beans and Broccoli

Preparation time 20 minutes,
cooking time 15 minutes

SERVES 4

300 g runner beans, stringed and shredded
150 g tenderstem broccoli

KEY SPICES
1 tsp cumin seeds
1 tsp brown mustard seeds
1 tsp red chilli flakes

WARMING SPICES
1 tsp fennel seeds
1 tsp fenugreek leaves
¼ tsp nigella seeds

OTHER SPICES
½ tsp asafoetida
2 tsp mango powder

WET INGREDIENTS
2 tbs groundnut oil
2 tsp pulped garlic
1 tsp pulped ginger
2 fresh green chillies, pierced
2 tsp white wine vinegar
2 tsp sundried tomato paste
1 tsp grated jaggery

6 - 8 fresh curry leaves
Sea salt to taste
Small bunch or coriander, roughly chopped

Place a large sauté pan on a low heat, add the oil and allow to warm.

Add the asafoetida and curry leaves, and allow to splutter. Then immediately add the key spices and warming spices, and stir well for 30 seconds.

Add the garlic, ginger and fresh green chillies, and continue to sauté for 1 minute.

Add the mango powder, white wine vinegar, sundried tomato paste and jaggery. Continue to cook for a further 2 minutes, adding a little water if the ingredients begin to stick to the pan.

Now turn the heat up high, add the runner beans, stir and sauté for 2 minutes.

Add the broccoli, stir well and cook for a further 5 minutes on a high heat.

I like to serve this dish 'al dente'. If you would prefer your vegetables to be a little more cooked, then simply sauté for a little longer.

Remove from the heat, add fresh coriander and sea salt to taste, stir and serve immediately.

My Dad grew up on a farm in Kenya, but the first time he saw broccoli was when he arrived in the UK. He was so intrigued with this vegetable that it was one of the very first dishes that he created, along with runner beans grown in our back garden. Broccoli is a fantastic source of vitamins K, and C. It's a really good source of dietary fibre, and a range of other key vitamins and nutrients.

Quick Spinach and Potatoes

Preparation time 10 minutes,
cooking time 20 minutes

SERVES 4

1 lb fresh or frozen chopped spinach
150 g baby new potatoes

KEY SPICES
1 tsp cumin seeds
1 tsp brown mustard seeds

WARMING SPICES
1 tsp fenugreek leaves
1 tsp fennel seeds

OTHER SPICES
¼ tsp asafoetida

WET INGREDIENTS
2 tbs unsalted butter or vegetable oil
2 tsp pulped garlic
1 tsp pulped ginger
2 fresh green chillies, pierced
2 tbs lemon juice
140 ml water

Sea salt to taste

GARNISH
Small bunch of coriander, chopped
Zest of one small lemon

Place a sauté pan on a low heat, add the butter or oil and allow to warm, then add the asafoetida and allow to sizzle.

Immediately add the key spices and warming spices.

Mix well, then add the garlic, ginger and green chillies.

Stir well and sauté for 2 minutes.

Add the spinach, potatoes, lemon juice, water and sea salt to taste.

Stir, place the lid on the pan and cook for 15 minutes or until the potatoes are cooked through.

Remove from the heat, add the fresh coriander and lemon zest, and stir.

'We always had plenty of spinach and potatoes growing in the back garden, and we'd serve this dish with delicious makki di roti (corn flour bread) which is gluten free too. Dad, in full Popeye mode, would sometimes give us leftover spinach and potatoes with a crispy paratha before we went to school, telling us how clever and strong spinach would make us. Later on I discovered that it has anti-inflammatory and anti-cancerous properties, and helps prevent cataracts and macular degeneration. Dad was always right.'

Messing about in the garden with my nieces,
who love fresh ingredients as much as I do.

MEAT

This very old pan is what my Dad used to warm his spices in. He said "Anjula, there's no need to roast your spices for too long. Just teasing them with a little warmth will begin to release the oils, leaving most of their magic to mix in".

Beef with Spinach

Serves 4

Preparation time 30 minutes, cooking time 90 minutes. Marinate overnight.

500 g beef sirloin, diced

FOR THE MARINADE
3 tbs unsweetened natural yogurt
1 tbs fresh raw papaya skin, grated
1 tbs fresh lemon juice
1 tsp pulped garlic
1 tsp pulped ginger

KEY SPICES
1 Indian bay leaf
1 1 inch piece of cassia bark

½ tsp turmeric powder
1 tsp red chilli flakes

1 tsp brown mustard seeds
1 tsp cumin seeds
1 tsp coriander seeds, crushed

WARMING SPICES
4 green cardamoms, lightly bashed
1 tsp fenugreek leaves, soaked in 2 tbs of hot water
1 tsp fennel seeds

WET INGREDIENTS
3 tbs coconut oil
2 large banana shallots, finely diced
400 g good chopped tinned tomatoes
1 tbs white wine vinegar
1 tsp pulped garlic
1 tsp pulped ginger
2-3 green chillies, pierced
330 ml pure coconut water
300 g baby spinach, washed and roughly chopped

Rock salt to taste

GARNISH
Small bunch of coriander including the stalks, finely chopped
Zest of a small lemon
1 tsp fresh horseradish, grated

Place the beef in a large bowl, add all the marinade ingredients, stir really well and make sure that all the meat is well coated. Place cling film over the bowl and marinate in the fridge overnight.

Remove the meat from the fridge, set aside and bring to room temperature

Take a large sauté pan and place on a low heat. Add the coconut oil and allow to warm through, then add the Indian bay leaf and cassia bark and stir for 30 seconds.

Add the shallots and sauté for 5 minutes.

Add the turmeric powder, red chilli flakes and salt to taste, then sauté for 5 minutes.

Add the brown mustard seeds and sauté for 2 minutes, then stir in the tomatoes and white wine vinegar and sauté for a further 10 minutes.

Add the cumin seeds, crushed coriander seeds, garlic, ginger and pierced green chillies. Sauté until the oil starts to appear on the surface and the whole mixture looks like a paste.

Add the beef, stir really well, turn the heat to medium and sauté for 5 minutes.

Once the beef changes colour, add the coconut water, bring to the boil and then immediately reduce to a simmer and place the lid on the pan.

Allow the beef to cook long and slow for about 30 minutes. In the meantime take a small dry frying pan, set on a low heat, add the warming spices and gently warm through for 1 minute. Remove from the heat and set aside.

Add the chopped spinach and the warming spices and stir.

Place the lid back on the pan, then sauté for a further 15 minutes or until the beef is tender.

Remove from the heat, stir in the chopped coriander, lime zest and horseradish, then place the lid on the pan and allow the garnish to infuse into the meat for 10 minutes.

Serve with a bowl of steamed basmati rice.

Remember to count your cardamoms in and count them out again before serving.

It was pretty rare that My Dad and I cooked with beef. Our neighbour, Mr Mayo, provided the unlikely prompt for this dish. He asked why he had never tasted any of our dishes with beef. This dish was our response.

Spinach and Chicken

Preparation time 30 minutes, cooking time 60 minutes. Marinate overnight

SERVES 4

750 g boneless skinless chicken thighs, cut into bite size pieces

FOR THE MARINADE
½ tsp ajwain seeds
1 tsp crushed coriander seeds

5 tbs natural yogurt
½ tsp turmeric powder
1 tsp pulped ginger
1 tsp pulped garlic

KEY SPICES
1 tsp cumin seeds
1 tsp coriander seeds
½ tsp brown mustard seeds

1 1 inch piece of cassia bark
1 Indian bay leaf

½ tsp turmeric powder
1 tsp red chilli flakes

WARMING SPICES
6 green cardamoms, lightly bashed
2 black cardamoms, lightly bashed
2 tbs fenugreek leaves, soaked in 4 tbs of hot water

WET INGREDIENTS
2 tbs vegetable oil
2 onions, finely chopped
4 medium sized fresh tomatoes, chopped
2 tsp pulped garlic
2 tsp pulped ginger
2 green chillies, slit lengthways
300 g frozen whole leaf spinach, thawed and chopped
100 ml water
1 tbs fresh lemon juice

1 tsp grated jaggery
Salt flakes or Himalayan rock salt to taste
Small bunch of fresh coriander, coarsely chopped

From the marinade list, take the ajwain seeds and crushed coriander seeds, and roast gently in a dry pan until fragrant, which should take about 1 minute. Set aside.

Place the chicken thighs in a large bowl and add the remaining marinade ingredients as well as the roasted ajwain and coriander seeds. Coat the chicken well, cover and place in the fridge overnight.

Remove the chicken from the fridge, and allow to come up to room temperature.

Place the warming spices, except for the soaked fenugreek leaves, in a dry pan on a low heat, and gently roast for 1 minute. Set aside.

In the same pan, still on a low heat, warm through the cumin seeds, coriander seeds and brown mustard seeds until fragrant. This should take 1 minute. Remove from the heat, add to the pestle and mortar and grind coarsely.

Take a large sauté pan, add the oil and warm on a low heat. Then add the onions, cassia bark and Indian bay leaf. Sauté for 5 minutes.

Add the turmeric powder and red chilli flakes, stir and cook for a further 2 minutes.

Add the chopped tomatoes, jaggery and salt to taste, and continue to sauté for at least a further 10 minutes, stirring occasionally.

By cooking these ingredients for a little longer, your curry will definitely taste better.

Now add the garlic, ginger and green chillies, and continue to cook for 2 minutes.

Add the contents of the pestle and mortar, stir well, and continue to fry until you see that the mixture resembles a paste, and the oil starts to separate from the onions and tomatoes.

Add the chicken, coat well, then add all of the warming spices.

Cook for 7 minutes, add the chopped spinach and water, bring to the boil and then reduce to a low simmer for 25-30 minutes with the lid on.

Remove from the heat, then add the lemon juice and fresh coriander.

Remember to count your cardamoms in and count them out again before serving.

This dish is a favourite in my home, and one of the most requested dishes when I cater. I love the clean taste of this recipe. Every mouthful really does make you feel good.

Chicken with Sorrel

Preparation time 30 minutes, cooking time 70 minutes

SERVES 4

750 g chicken thighs, on the bone
50 g fresh sorrel, washed and finely chopped

KEY SPICES
1 tsp cumin seeds
1 tsp coriander seeds
1 tsp brown mustard seeds
½ tsp black peppercorns

1 1 inch piece of cassia bark
1 Indian bay leaf

1 tsp turmeric powder
1 tsp red chilli flakes

WARMING SPICES
4 green cardamoms, lightly bashed
1 black cardamom, lightly bashed
1 tsp fenugreek leaves, soaked in 2 tbs of hot water

WET INGREDIENTS
2 tbs groundnut oil
2 large onions, chopped finely
200 ml of good quality tinned chopped tomatoes
1 tsp poppy seeds, dry roasted and ground into a paste with a little hot water
2 tsp pulped garlic
2 tsp pulped ginger
2-4 fresh green chillies, pierced
140 ml water

Salt flakes to taste
1 tsp grated jaggery
Small bunch of fresh coriander, chopped

Take a small dry frying pan, set on a low heat, and warm through the cumin seeds, coriander seeds, brown mustard seeds and black peppercorns until fragrant. This should take 1 minute, as you are just trying to tease the oil out of the spices. Remove from the heat, add to the pestle and mortar and grind coarsely.

Take a large sauté pan, add the oil and warm on a low heat. Then add the onions, cassia bark, bay leaf and salt to taste. Sauté for 5 minutes.

Add the turmeric powder and red chilli flakes, stir and sauté for 2 minutes.

Add the chopped tomatoes, poppy seed paste and jaggery, and continue to sauté for a further 10 minutes, stirring occasionally.

By cooking these ingredients for a little longer, your curry will definitely taste better.

Now add the garlic, ginger and green chillies, and sauté for 2 minutes.

Add the contents of the pestle and mortar, stir well, and sauté for about 10 minutes, until you see that the mixture resembles a paste.

If the paste becomes a little dry and sticks to the pan, then just add a little water whenever you need, to help you achieve the required consistency.

Heat the black and green cardamoms in a small dry pan until fragrant. Set aside.

Add the chicken thighs, coat and stir well, turn the heat up to high and seal the chicken for 10 minutes.

Add the sorrel, stir in the black and green cardamoms, soaked fenugreek and water. Bring to the boil, then immediately reduce to a simmer.

Place the lid on the pan, cook for 25 minutes, or until the thighs are cooked through.

Switch off the heat, add the fresh coriander including the stalks, and serve with rice.

Remember to count your cardamoms in and count them out again before serving.

Sorrel, with its fresh, crisp, green leaves and tangy after tones is a superfood packed with vitamins A, B and C and containing iron, magnesium, potassium, and calcium. My Dad used to say that chicken and sorrel were a perfect match.

Chicken Curry

Preparation time 30 minutes, cooking time 75 minutes. Marinate overnight.

Serves 4

350 g boneless and skinless chicken thighs, cut into bite size pieces
350 g boneless and skinless chicken breast, cut into bite size pieces

For the Marinade
150 g natural yogurt
Juice of one freshly squeezed lemon
1 tsp pulped garlic
1 tsp pulped ginger
1 tsp tomato paste
2 tbs tamarind pulp

Key Spices
1 tsp cumin seeds
1 tsp coriander seeds
1 tsp brown mustard seeds

1 1 inch piece of cassia bark
1 Indian bay leaf
¼ tsp turmeric powder
1 tsp red chilli flakes

Warming Spices
1 tsp fenugreek leaves, soaked in 2 tbs hot water
4 green cardamoms, lightly bashed
2 cloves

Wet Ingredients
4 tbs vegetable oil
2 medium onions, finely chopped
400 g good quality tinned chopped tomatoes
1 tsp pulped garlic
1 tsp pulped ginger
2-4 fresh finger green chillies, pierced (add less for a milder curry)
6-8 curry leaves
140 ml water (more if you prefer your sauce to be not as thick)
2 tsp tamarind pulp

1 tsp jaggery, grated

Garnish
Small bunch of fresh coriander, chopped
Zest of one lemon

Place the chicken thighs and breasts in a large bowl, add the marinade ingredients, stir and coat well. Cover the bowl and place in the fridge overnight.

Remove from the fridge, set aside, and allow the chicken to come to room temperature.

Take a small dry frying pan, set on a low heat, and warm through the cumin seeds, coriander seeds and brown mustard seeds. This should only take 1 minute. Remove from the heat, add to the pestle and mortar and grind coarsely.

Take a large sauté pan, add the oil and warm on a low heat. Then add the onions, cassia bark and bay leaf. Sauté for 5 minutes.

Add the turmeric and red chilli flakes, stir and cook for a further 2 minutes.

Add the chopped tomatoes and jaggery, and continue to sauté for at least a further 10 minutes, stirring occasionally.

By cooking these ingredients for a little longer, your curry will definitely taste better.

Now add the garlic, ginger and green chillies, and continue to cook for 2 minutes.

Add the contents of the pestle and mortar, stir well, and continue to fry until you see that the mixture resembles a paste, and the oil starts to separate from the onions and tomatoes.

If the ingredients start to become a little dry or the spices start to burn, simply add a little water.

Add the marinated chicken and fresh curry leaves (rip these into smaller pieces).

Turn the heat up to medium, stir really well, and allow the chicken to seal for at least 5 minutes, stirring frequently.

Add the water and bring to the boil, then immediately reduce to a simmer. Add the soaked fenugreek leaves, green cardamoms, cloves and tamarind pulp, and place the lid on the pan.

Cook for 25 minutes or until the chicken is tender, and the sauce is thick.

Remove from the heat, and stir in the fresh coriander and lemon zest.
Leave for 5 minutes before serving.

Remember to count your cardamoms and cloves in and count them out again before serving.

Coconut Chicken Strips

Preparation time 4 hours and 30 minutes, cooking time 30 minutes

SERVES 4

4 chicken breasts

KEY SPICES
1 tsp cumin seeds
1 tsp coriander seeds
1 tsp brown mustard seeds
1 tsp black peppercorns
2 tsp red chilli flakes

WARMING SPICES
1 star anise
½ tsp fennel seeds
1 tsp mango powder

OTHER INGREDIENTS
2 tbs lemon juice
3 tbs buttermilk
Salt flakes to taste
Small bunch of coriander, finely chopped
115 g coconut flour
2 eggs
150 g unsweetened coconut flakes
Coconut spray

Place all of the spices (key spices and warming spices) into a large dry frying pan and roast until fragrant.

Either pound these to a fine powder in the pestle and mortar, or use a grinder. Then place in a large bowl and set aside.

Take one chicken breast at a time, place between two sheets of cling film and pound the chicken flat and evenly with a rolling pin.

Cut the chicken into thick strips and place into the large bowl with the spices, lemon juice, buttermilk and salt.

Toss and coat the chicken well, and refrigerate for at least 4 hours.

Remove the chicken from the fridge, and bring to room temperature.

Add the chopped coriander, including the stalks, and mix well.

Line a baking sheet with parchment paper, and pre-heat the oven to gas mark 6, 400°F (200°C).

Place the coconut flour on a large plate. Set aside.

Whisk the eggs in a large sized bowl. Set aside.

Put the coconut flakes on a large sized plate. Set aside.

Carefully dip the chicken strips first into the coconut flour, then into the eggs, and finally into the coconut flakes.

Place the chicken strips gently on the baking sheet lined with parchment paper. Spray the chicken strips with a little coconut spray.

Place in the oven and bake for about 15 minutes, or until the strips are browned.

Serve with peach and roasted shallot chutney (see page 184).

Chicken Thighs
with Pomegranate

Preparation time 30 minutes, cooking time 30 minutes. For best results marinate overnight.

SERVES 4

16 chicken thighs, on the bone and the skin left on

KEY SPICES
2 tsp cumin seeds
2 tsp coriander seeds
1 1 inch piece of cassia bark

WARMING SPICES
2 tsp fenugreek leaves
2 cloves

OTHER SPICES
¼ tsp nutmeg, freshly grated

WET INGREDIENTS
100 ml pomegranate molasses
8 spring onions, finely chopped
3 tsp pulped garlic
3 tbs natural yogurt
2 tbs coconut oil
3 tbs white wine vinegar

1 tbs grated jaggery
Sea salt to taste

GARNISH
Small bunch of coriander, chopped finely
Zest of one large lemon
Handful of fresh pomegranate seeds

Place all the key spices and warming spices in a dry frying pan and warm for 1 minute. Remove from the heat, add to the pestle and mortar and grind to a powder. Set aside.

Apart from the garnish ingredients take all the remaining ingredients, add to a blender and create a smooth marinade.

Remove from the blender, add to a large mixing bowl along with the contents of the pestle and mortar and stir really well. Add the chicken thighs to the bowl and coat them really well.

Cover the bowl, and for best results marinate overnight.

Remove the bowl from the fridge and allow the thighs to come to room temperature.

Pre-heat the oven to gas mark 190 C, 375 F or gas mark 5, then place the thighs on an oven proof dish. Try not to crowd the thighs as you want the skin to become golden and crisp, and it will take longer if they don't have enough space between them.

Roast for 25 - 30 minutes, check the thighs are cooked all the way through and remove from the oven.

Mix together the fresh coriander and lemon zest, gently stir and coat the thighs, then sprinkle with fresh pomegranate.

Serve hot or cold.

Growing up, we always had children from our street in the back garden and Dad would feed anyone who was hungry. Some of the younger children would find the food a little spicy, so Dad came up with this chicken dish, made without chillies.

Roast Poussin with Ajwain seeds and Baby Figs

Preparation time 30 minutes, cooking time 60 minutes. Marinate overnight.

SERVES 4

4 poussins (young chickens)

KEY SPICES
½ tsp cumin seeds
½ tsp crushed coriander seeds
½ tsp crushed black peppercorns
1 tsp red chilli flakes

WARMING SPICES
6 green cardamoms, lightly bashed
1 tsp fennel seeds
1 tsp fenugreek leaves, soaked in 2 tbs of hot water

OTHER SPICES
2 tsp ajwain seeds

FOR THE MARINADE
8 baby figs, finely chopped
4 tbs lemon juice
2 tsp pulped garlic
2 tsp pulped ginger
2 fresh mild red chillies, chopped roughly
3 dry Kashmiri chillies
4 tbs groundnut oil
1 tbs sundried tomato paste
8 banana shallots, peeled and halved
4 tbs thick natural yogurt
1 tbs roasted gram flour
2 fresh tomatoes, roughly chopped
1 tsp grated jaggery
2 oz. clarified butter
1 tbs pulped kiwi fruit

GARNISH
4 wedges of fresh lemon
Small bunch of fresh coriander including stalks, chopped

4 pieces of butcher's string

Preheat the oven to 220°C/Fan oven 200C/gas 7. A 450g poussin serves one, and needs quick roasting.

Place a dry frying pan on a low heat and roast the key spices, warming spices and other spices until fragrant, then remove from the heat.

Then remove the seeds from the green cardamom and disregard the husk.

Place the cardamom seeds, along with all of the other roasted spices and the marinade, into a grinder to create a smooth paste.

Place the poussins in a large deep roasting tray and smother and coat them inside and out with the marinade. Cover and place in the fridge overnight.

Remove the poussins from the fridge, and bring to room temperature.

Place a lemon wedge inside each poussin, tie the legs together with butcher's string, and roast in the oven for 35-40 minutes ensuring that you baste at least twice during the roasting period.

Remove from the oven, and allow to rest for 15 minutes before serving.

Garnish with the fresh coriander leaves and stalks.

Serve with a chutney of your choice.

This is a dish which provides some variety when I cater, and has persuaded people who thought they didn't like Indian food that actually they do. Baby figs add a really special flavour to this dish.

Lamb and Amla
(Gooseberry)

Preparation time 20 minutes, cooking time 1 hour and 40 minutes. Marinate overnight.

SERVES 4-6

700 g lean lamb neck fillet or shoulder, cut into 5 cm cubes

FOR THE MARINADE
200 g natural yogurt
1 tsp pulped garlic
2 tsp pulped ginger
2 tbs raw papaya skin, grated
Juice and zest of one lemon

KEY SPICES
1 Indian bay leaf
1 1 inch piece of cassia bark

1 tsp turmeric powder

1 tsp cumin seeds
2 tsp crushed coriander seeds
1 tsp brown mustard seeds
4 whole Kashmiri chillies

WARMING SPICES
1 tsp fennel seeds
1 tsp nigella seeds
4 green cardamoms, lightly bashed
1 black cardamom, lightly bashed
2 cloves
2 tsp fenugreek leaves

OTHER SPICES
1 tsp mango powder

WET INGREDIENTS
4 tbs vegetable oil
2 medium onions, finely diced
300 g good chopped tinned tomatoes
2 tsp pulped garlic
1 tsp pulped ginger
2 -3 green chillies, pierced
300 ml water
400 g fresh gooseberries
6 fresh curry leaves (optional)
Small bunch of fresh coriander, chopped

1 tsp grated jaggery
Sea salt to taste

Place the lamb in a large bowl, add the marinade ingredients, mix well, cover and place in the fridge overnight.

NB Please ensure that you bring the lamb up to room temperature before adding to the pan.

Heat the oil in a large pan on a low to medium heat.

Add the onions and sauté for 2 minutes.

Add the Indian bay leaf, cassia bark and salt to taste. Sauté for 2 minutes.

Add the turmeric powder and continue to sauté for 2 minutes,

Add the tomatoes and jaggery and continue to sauté for 5 minutes.

Add the cumin seeds, crushed coriander seeds, brown mustard seeds and Kashmiri chillies and sauté for 2 minutes.

Add the garlic, ginger and green chillies and sauté for 5 minutes.

Reduce the heat to low, and allow to cook for at least 15 minutes or until the oil appears at the sides or on top of the ingredients.

Now add the lamb and increase the heat to high. Cook for a further 15 minutes, add the water and simmer for at least 30 minutes. Remove the lid and add the gooseberries, warming spices and fresh curry leaves. Stir well and place the lid on the pan for a further 15 minutes.

Remove from the heat, stir in mango powder and fresh coriander. Season with salt to taste.

Allow to sit for 5 minutes before serving.

Enjoy with Rumali roti.

Remember to count the cardamoms and cloves in and count them out again before serving.

Keema Peas

Preparation time 30 minutes,
cooking time 80 minutes

SERVES 4

400 g lean minced lamb
150 g frozen garden peas

KEY SPICES
1 tsp cumin seeds
1 tsp coriander seeds
1 tsp brown mustard seeds
½ tsp black peppercorns

1 1 inch piece of cassia bark
1 Indian bay leaf

1 tsp turmeric powder
1 tsp red chilli flakes

WARMING SPICES
2 tsp fenugreek leaves, soaked in 4 tbs hot water
6 green cardamom, lightly bashed
1 black cardamom, lightly bashed
2 cloves

OTHER SPICES
½ tsp ajwain seeds

WET INGREDIENTS
2 tbs vegetable oil
2 medium onions, finely chopped
2 tsp pulped garlic
1 tsp pulped ginger
3 green chillies, pierced
200 g good quality chopped tinned tomatoes
1 tsp sundried tomato paste

1 tsp jaggery
Rock salt or salt flakes to taste
Small bunch of fresh coriander, chopped

Take a small dry frying pan, set on a low heat, and warm through the cumin seeds, coriander seeds, brown mustard seeds, black peppercorns and ajwain seeds until fragrant. This should take 1 minute, as you are just trying to tease the oil out of the spices. Remove from the heat, add to the pestle and mortar and grind coarsely.

Take a large sauté pan, add the oil and warm on a low heat. Then add the onions, cassia bark, Indian bay leaf and salt to taste. Sauté for 5 minutes.

Add the turmeric and red chilli flakes, stir and sauté for 2 minutes.

Add the chopped tomatoes, tomato paste and jaggery, and continue to sauté for a further 10 minutes, stirring occasionally.

By cooking these ingredients for a little longer, your curry will definitely taste better.

Now add the garlic, ginger and green chillies, and sauté for 2 minutes.

Add the contents of the pestle and mortar, stir well, and sauté for about 10 minutes, until you see that the mixture resembles a paste.

If the paste becomes a little dry and sticks to the pan, then just add a little water whenever you need, to help you achieve the required consistency.

Add in the minced lamb, stir and mix really well. Sauté on a medium heat for 5 minutes.

Add the warming spices, stir then cover, and cook over a low heat for 20 -25 minutes, stirring occasionally, until the lamb is cooked through.

Add the peas and cook on a high heat without the lid for 5 minutes.

Remove from the heat, put the lid on the pan, and leave for 10 minutes.

Add the chopped coriander, and serve with chapattis or rice.

Remember to count your cardamoms and cloves in and count them out again before serving.

When it comes to comfort food, this dish really does wrap you up with a big fat cuddle! Adding ajwain seeds, which should never be overused, takes this dish up another notch. Ajwain seeds have a bold flavour, rather like thyme or oregano, which lamb handles really well.

Kashmiri Lamb with Spinach

Preparation time 30 minutes, cooking time 2 hours. Marinate overnight. A little tip, you can buy fresh spinach and place it in the freezer. When you need it, remove from the freezer and crush the frozen leaves in the bag to save time chopping.

SERVES 4

750g lamb neck fillet, cut into cubes

FOR THE MARINADE
2 tbs natural yogurt
1 tbs fresh lemon juice
2 tbs raw papaya skin, grated
1 tsp pulped garlic
1 tsp pulped ginger
¼ tsp salt flakes

KEY SPICES
1 tsp cumin seeds
1 tsp coriander seeds
1 tsp brown mustard seeds
½ tsp black peppercorns

1 1 inch piece of cassia bark
1 Indian bay leaf

1 tsp turmeric powder
1 tsp red chilli flakes

WARMING SPICES
4 whole Kashmiri chillies
4 green cardamoms, lightly bashed
2 black cardamoms, lightly bashed
3 cloves
2 tsp fenugreek seeds, soaked in 4tbs hot water

Place the lamb in a large bowl.

Place all the marinade ingredients in a small blender, and create a paste to add to the lamb.

Mix and coat the lamb well with the marinade, cover the bowl, and place in the refrigerator overnight.

Remove the lamb from the fridge, and bring to room temperature. Pre heat the oven to 200 C (400 F) or gas mark 6.

Take the baby spinach leaves, (if frozen, crush them in the bag) and place in a bowl with the natural yogurt, mixing really well. Set aside.

Place the lamb in a large roasting tray, and roast for 15 minutes. Remove from the oven. Set aside.

Take a small dry frying pan, set on a low heat, and warm through the cumin seeds, coriander seeds, brown mustard seeds and black peppercorns until fragrant. This should take 1 minute, as you are just trying to tease the oil out of the spices. Remove from the heat, add to the pestle and mortar and grind coarsely.

Take a large sauté pan, add the oil and warm on a low heat. Then add the onions, cassia bark, Indian bay leaf, curry leaves (if using), Kashmiri chillies and salt to taste. Sauté for 5 minutes.

Add the turmeric powder and red chilli flakes, stir and sauté for 2 minutes.

Add the chopped tomatoes and jaggery, and continue to sauté for a further 10 minutes, stirring occasionally.

By cooking these ingredients for a little longer, your curry will definitely taste better.

Now add the garlic, ginger and green chillies, and sauté for 2 minutes.

Add the contents of the pestle and mortar, stir well, and sauté for about 10 minutes, until you see that the mixture resembles a paste.

If the paste becomes a little dry and sticks to the pan, then just add a little water whenever you need, to help you achieve the required consistency.

Add the lamb and turn the heat to high, to make sure that all the lamb is well coated. Cook on a high heat for 10 minutes, stirring frequently.

Add the water and bring up to the boil, then reduce to a very low simmer for 30 minutes, with the lid on.

400 g baby spinach leaves, fresh or frozen
50 g natural yogurt
4 tbs vegetable oil
2 large onions, finely chopped
200 g good quality tinned chopped tomatoes
1 tsp pulped garlic
1 tsp pulped ginger
2 green chillies, pierced (or you can add more or less)
280 ml water

Rock salt or salt flakes to taste
1 tsp jaggery, grated
6 curry leaves (optional)
Himalayan pink rock salt or sea salt flakes to taste
Small bunch of coriander, roughly chopped including stalks

In the meantime, take a dry frying pan, and on a medium heat dry roast the green cardamoms, black cardamoms and cloves, until fragrant.

Add the warming spices, soaked fenugreek, mixed spinach and yogurt. Stir really well, place the lid back on the pan, and cook for a further 20 minutes, or until the lamb is tender.

The slower you cook this dish, the better it will taste. You only need to stir once or twice during this stage.

There is a great tell-tale sign that will inform you that the lamb is almost ready. It is when most of the oil begins to appear on the surface, and it is a crimson glossy dark red colour.

Check that the lamb is tender. If it needs more time or you would like the sauce to be a little thicker, just cook without the lid on until you get the desired level of thickness.

Remove from the heat, add the chopped coriander and serve with hot chapattis.

Remember to count your cardamoms and cloves in and count them out again before serving.

This is a delicious dish which I use Kashmiri chillies in. One of my favourite mild chillies, with a stunning colour, full flavour and a fruity undertone.

Lamb Dhansak -
Made in a Slow Cooker

Preparation time 30 minutes,
cooking time 7 hours and 30 minutes.

SERVES 4

500 g lamb neck fillet, cut into bite sized
chunks
50 g red lentils

KEY SPICES
1 Indian bay leaf
1 1 inch piece of cassia bark
1 tsp red chilli flakes
1 tsp turmeric powder

1 tsp cumin seeds
1 tsp coriander seeds
½ tsp black peppercorns

WARMING SPICES
1 star anise
3 green cardamoms, lightly bashed
2 cloves
2 tsp fenugreek leaves, soaked in 2 tbs hot
water

WET INGREDIENTS
4 tbs vegetable oil
2 medium onions, chopped (for a great
curry, sauté your onions for a few minutes)
2 tsp white vinegar
4 small fresh tomatoes, chopped
1 small aubergine, chopped
125 g pumpkin, chopped
1 tsp pulped garlic
1 tsp pulped ginger
3 - 4 green chillies, pierced
2 oz unsalted butter

1 tsp grated jaggery
Rock salt or salt flakes to taste
570 ml hot water, from the kettle
Small bunch of fresh coriander, chopped
Zest of one small lemon

Wash the lentils thoroughly under a cold running tap, and then add to the slow cooker.

Heat a large frying pan with 2 tbs of oil on a medium heat. Brown the lamb in two batches, and place in the slow cooker.

In the same frying pan, add the onions, bay leaf, cassia bark, red chilli flakes and turmeric powder, and sauté on a medium heat for 5 minutes. Then add to the slow cooker, along with the vinegar, tomatoes, aubergine, pumpkin, garlic, ginger, green chillies, butter, jaggery, and the remaining oil.

Heat a small dry pan, and roast the remaining key spices - cumin seeds, coriander seeds and black peppercorns until fragrant.

Remove from the heat, place in a pestle and mortar, coarsely grind, and add to the slow cooker along with the hot water.

Place the lid on the slow cooker, and cook for 5 hours on the lowest setting.

In the meantime dry roast the warming spices, apart from the soaked fenugreek leaves, until fragrant. Set aside.

Check the lamb after 5 hours, add the roasted warming spices, along with the soaked fenugreek leaves, and replace the lid.

Cook for a further 2 hours.

If you'd like the sauce to be a little thicker, set the slow cooker on high, and cook for a further 10 to 15 minutes without the lid on.

Switch off the cooker, add the fresh coriander, lemon zest and salt to taste. Remember to remove the star anise, cardamoms and cloves from the lamb.

Serve with rice.

This is definitely worth the time invested in perfecting. The hot, sweet and sour combinations make this really enjoyable. It's a really popular dish, originating from the Parsi community.

Lamb in Indian Pickling Spices

Preparation time 30 minutes, cooking time 90 minutes. Marinate overnight.

SERVES 4

500g lamb neck fillet, cut into cubes

FOR THE MARINADE
2 tbs natural yogurt
2 tbs raw papaya skin
¼ tsp salt flakes
½ tsp asafoetida
2 tsp fenugreek leaves

KEY SPICES
1 tsp cumin seeds
1 tsp coriander seeds
1 tsp brown mustard seeds
½ tsp black peppercorns

1 1 inch piece of cassia bark
1 Indian bay leaf

1 tsp turmeric powder
1 tsp red chilli flakes

WARMING SPICES
1 tsp fennel seeds
4 green cardamoms, lightly bashed
2 black cardamoms, lightly bashed
3 cloves

OTHER SPICES
¼ tsp nigella seeds
4 whole dry Kashmiri chillies
2 tsp mango powder

Place the lamb in a large bowl.

Place all the marinade ingredients in a small blender, and create a paste to add to the lamb.

Mix and coat the lamb well, cover the bowl, and place in the refrigerator overnight.

Remove the lamb from the fridge, and bring to room temperature.

Take a small dry frying pan, set on a low heat, and warm through the cumin seeds, coriander seeds, brown mustard seeds and black peppercorns until fragrant. This should take 1 minute, as you are just trying to tease the oil out of the spices. Remove from the heat, add to the pestle and mortar and grind coarsely.

Take a large sauté pan, add the oil and warm on a low heat. Then add the onions, cassia bark, Indian bay leaf and salt to taste. Sauté for 5 minutes.

Add the turmeric powder and red chilli flakes, stir and sauté for 2 minutes. Add the chopped tomatoes, jaggery and curry leaves, and continue to sauté for a further 10 minutes, stirring occasionally.

By cooking these ingredients for a little longer, your curry will definitely taste better.

Now add the garlic, ginger and green chillies, and sauté for 2 minutes.

Add the contents of the pestle and mortar, stir well, and sauté for about 10 minutes, until you see that the mixture resembles a paste.

If the paste becomes a little dry and sticks to the pan, then just add a little water whenever you need, to help you achieve the required consistency.

Whilst keeping a close watch on the large sauté pan, take a small dry frying pan, set it on a low heat, add the warming spices and roast until fragrant.

Add the warming spices to the large sauté pan, stir well.

Add the lamb and turn the heat to high to make sure that all the lamb is well coated, cooking on a high heat for 10 minutes, stirring frequently.

Add the water and bring up to the boil, then reduce to a very low simmer, and cook until the lamb is tender.

After 75 minutes, add the lemon juice, and then cook for another 15 minutes.

The slower you cook this dish, the better it will taste. You only need to stir once or twice during this time.

There is a great tell-tale sign that will inform you that the lamb is almost ready.

4 tbs vegetable oil
2 large onions, finely chopped
2 tsp pulped garlic
2 tsp pulped ginger
2 green chillies, pierced
200 g good quality tinned chopped
tomatoes
280 ml water
Juice of 1 small lemon
Small bunch of coriander, roughly chopped
including stalks

1 tsp grated jaggery
6 curry leaves (optional)
Himalayan pink rock salt or sea salt flakes
to taste

It is when most of the oil begins to appear right on top of the surface, and is a crimson glossy dark red colour.

Check that the lamb is tender. If it needs more time or you would like the sauce to be a little thicker, just cook without the lid on, until you get the desired level of thickness.

Remove from the heat, add the chopped coriander and serve with hot chapattis.

Remember to count your cardamoms and cloves in and count them out again before serving.

Papaya is one of the best tenderisers for red meat. It is important to know that the enzymes in the papaya skin which are responsible for breaking down the fibres in the meat only begin to react when they are heated.

Lamb Shanks
Cooked in Yogurt

Preparation time 30 minutes, cooking time
4 hours and 40 minutes

Serves 6

6 medium size lamb shanks

Key Spices
1 tsp cumin seeds
1 tsp coriander seeds
1 tsp brown mustard seeds
½ tsp black peppercorns

1 1 inch piece of cassia bark
1 Indian bay leaf

1 tsp turmeric powder
1 tsp red chilli flakes

Warming Spices
8 cardamoms, lightly bashed
2 black cardamom, lightly bashed
1 tsp fennel seeds
8 fresh curry leaves
2 tsp fenugreek leaves, soaked in 4 tbs hot
water

Other Spices
1 tsp ajwain seeds
1 tsp asafoetida
6 Kashmiri whole chillies

Wet Ingredients
4 tbs groundnut oil
2 large onions, chopped finely
300 g good quality chopped tinned
tomatoes
2 tsp pulped garlic
2 tsp pulped ginger
4 green chillies, pierced
250 ml natural yogurt, whisked with ¼ pint
of water
1 small bunch coriander, chopped including
the stalks
1 small bunch fresh mint, chopped

1 tsp jaggery
Rock salt or salt flakes to taste

Take a small dry frying pan, set on a low heat, and warm through the cumin seeds, coriander seeds, brown mustard seeds, black peppercorns and ajwain seeds until fragrant. This should take 1 minute, as you are just trying to tease the oil out of the spices. Remove from the heat, add to the pestle and mortar and grind coarsely.

Take a large sauté pan, add the oil and warm on a low heat. Then add the onions, cassia bark, Indian bay leaf, asafoetida, Kashmiri chillies and salt to taste. Sauté for 5 minutes.

Add the turmeric and red chilli flakes, stir and sauté for 2 minutes.

Add the chopped tomatoes and jaggery, and continue to sauté for a further 10 minutes, stirring occasionally.

By cooking these ingredients for a little longer, your curry will definitely taste better.

Now add the garlic, ginger and green chillies, and sauté for 2 minutes.

Add the contents of the pestle and mortar, stir well, and sauté for about 10 minutes, until you see that the mixture resembles a paste.

If the paste becomes a little dry and sticks to the pan, then just add a little water whenever you need, to help you achieve the required consistency.

Add the lamb shanks and coat well with all the spices, cook on a high heat for 5 minutes.

Add the whisked yogurt and water and bring to the boil.

Reduce to a very low simmer, place the lid on the pan and cook for 4 hours.

In the last hour of cooking, take a dry frying pan and roast the warming spices until fragrant, and add to the lamb shanks.

Once the shanks are completely tender and are falling off the bone, switch off the heat. Remember to count in the cardamoms and count them out again.

Add the fresh coriander and mint.

Serve with rice or chapattis.

This is a perfect dish for guests. It is best cooked long and slow, whilst you get on with other things. It features smoky black cardamom and is finished with fresh mint.

Pulled Lamb with Fiery Mint Chutney

Preparation time 30 minutes, cooking time 4 hours and 40 minutes. Marinate overnight.

SERVES 4

1.5 kg boneless shoulder lamb, butterflied (ask your butcher to do this, and to score it too)

KEY SPICES
1 tsp turmeric powder
2 tsp red chilli flakes
2 Indian bay leaves
2 1 inch pieces of cassia bark
2 tsp cumin seeds
1 tbs coriander seeds
1 tsp black peppercorns
1 tsp brown mustard seeds
1 tbs paprika

WARMING SPICES
8 green cardamoms
2 black cardamoms
2 cloves
1 tsp fennel seeds
2 tbs fenugreek leaves

OTHER SPICES
2 tbs mango powder

WET INGREDIENTS
2 large onions, sliced
250 ml white wine vinegar
2 tbs Worcestershire sauce
2 tbs dark brown soft sugar
2 tbs grated jaggery
4 tsp pulped garlic
2 tsp pulped ginger
4 fresh mild green chillies minced (you can remove the membrane and seeds if you prefer a milder version)
150 g sundried tomato paste
4 large ripe tomatoes, chopped finely
4 tbs raw papaya skin (try not to miss this ingredient out as it's the tenderiser for the lamb)
4 tbs groundnut oil or vegetable oil

GARNISH
1 small bunch of coriander, chopped
1 small bunch of mint, chopped
Zest and juice of one lime

You are going to love this recipe - take a large frying pan set on a low heat, add all the key spices to the pan and gently warm through for 1 minute.

Remove from the heat, place in a pestle and mortar, grind to a fine powder and add to a large mixing bowl.

This is the best bit - take all of the wet ingredients and the mango powder and add to the bowl. Mix really well, add the lamb and coat it with all the other ingredients.

Cover the bowl and place in the fridge overnight.

Remove from the fridge and bring to room temperature for at least 30 minutes.

Pre-heat the oven to 140 C, 280 F or gas mark 1, then place the lamb including all the marinade in an oven proof dish. Cover with foil and cook for 4 hours.

In the meantime take a small dry frying pan and warm through the warming spices for 1 minute.

Remove from the heat, bash the green cardamoms and black cardamoms in a pestle and mortar, remove their husks and place the seeds back into the pestle and mortar. Grind to a fine powder along with the cloves, fennel and fenugreek Set aside.

Remove the foil, add the ground warming spices to the lamb.

Cook for a further 30 minutes without the foil on, or until the meat just pulls away with a fork.

Remove from the oven, add the coriander, mint, lime juice and zest.

Serve with fresh chapattis and the fiery mint chutney (see page 177).

FISH

My Dad used to say "Anjula, there's an art to making fish dishes. Too much spice will ruin the fish".

Gluten-Free Fish Balls with Fresh Red Chillies and Coconut

Preparation time 2 hours and 20 minutes (includes 2 hours refrigeration), cooking time 20 minutes

SERVES 4

FOR THE FISH BALLS

700 g of any firm white fish fillet. I used haddock for this recipe
450 g deveined raw prawns

1 tsp cumin seeds
½ tsp fennel seeds
¼ tsp white pepper
1 tsp grated jaggery
1 tsp pulped ginger
1 tsp red chilli flakes
2 tsp mango powder
2 fresh green chillies, minced (feel free to remove membrane and seeds for a milder taste)
Sea salt to taste
1 tsp coconut oil
Stalks from a small bunch of fresh coriander, chopped finely
Juice and zest of one lime

Place the fish and prawns on a kitchen towel and pat them dry.

Place the prawns and fish in a food processor. Using the pulse button, purée the fish until it looks a little like a paste.

Remove from the processor and place in a large bowl.

Warm the cumin seeds and fennel seeds in a small dry frying pan for 1 minute. Add to a pestle and mortar and grind to a powder.

Add the contents of the pestle and mortar to the bowl, along with the remaining ingredients and mix thoroughly.

To make the fish balls, wet your hands, take enough paste to form a shape which is the size of a golf ball. You should be able to make approximately 16 fish balls from this recipe.

Once all the fish balls have been made, place in a bowl, cover with cling film and place in the fridge for at least two hours.

A delicious fish curry which takes a little time to prepare, and is written in two parts for you. It is a great dish for entertaining, as you can make the fish balls the night before. My Dad used to make this dish with fish fingers, which I also did when my children were young.

KEY SPICES
1 tsp cumin seeds
1 tsp brown mustard seeds
1 tsp turmeric powder
1 tsp red chilli flakes

WARMING SPICES
½ tsp fennel seeds
¼ tsp nigella seeds

WET INGREDIENTS
1 large onion thinly sliced
2 tbs coconut oil
2 tsp pulped garlic
1 tsp pulped ginger
2 tsp sundried tomato paste
2-3 birds eye red chillies, pierced (I use 3, but you can reduce)
220 ml coconut milk
180 ml water

6-8 fresh curry leaves, chopped finely (optional) I use scissor to cut curry leaves, as I find it easier than using a knife
Sea salt to taste
1 tsp grated jaggery

GARNISH
Small bunch of fresh coriander, chopped roughly

Remove the fish balls from the fridge. Add 1 tbs of the coconut oil to a large pan, allow to heat and shallow fry the fish balls in batches until a light golden-brown.

Remove and place on absorbent kitchen paper. Set aside.

In the same pan, add the remaining coconut oil, allow to warm and then add the curry leaves. Allow to splutter, then add the thinly sliced onions and sauté for about 8 minutes until golden-brown.

Add the key spices and warming spices. Sauté for 1 minute.

Add the garlic and ginger and sauté for 1 minute.

Add the sundried tomato paste and birds eye chillies. Stir and sauté for 1 minute.

Add the coconut milk, water, sea salt and jaggery. Bring to the boil and then immediately reduce to a simmer.

Add the fish balls and simmer for 10 minutes with the pan covered.

Remove from the heat, add fresh coriander and serve with boiled rice.

Goan Fish Curry

Preparation time 20 minutes,
cooking time 50 minutes

SERVES 4

700 g firm white fish (I like to use haddock
or hake)

KEY SPICES
1 tsp cumin seeds
1 tsp coriander seeds
1 tsp brown mustard seeds

1 tsp turmeric powder

WARMING SPICES
2 star anise
1 tsp fenugreek leaves, soaked in 2 tbs hot
water

OTHER SPICES
4-6 dry red whole Kashmiri chillies

WET INGREDIENTS
3 tbs coconut oil
2 small onions, finely chopped
1 tbs white wine vinegar
2 fresh ripe tomatoes, finely chopped
2 tsp pulped garlic
1 tsp pulped ginger
2 fresh green chillies, pierced
1 small raw green mango, grated (if you
struggle to buy these, use 2 tbs tamarind
paste)
2 tsp sundried tomato paste
400 ml coconut milk
100 ml water

8-10 curry leaves, ripped
Sea salt to taste
1 tbs grated jaggery

GARNISH
Small bunch of fresh coriander, chopped
Juice and zest of one lime

Place a small dry frying pan on a low heat, allow to warm, add the cumin seeds, coriander seeds and brown mustard seeds, and warm for 1 minute.

Remove from the heat, add to a pestle and mortar, grind coarsely and set aside.

Place a sauté pan on a low heat, add the coconut oil and allow to warm, then add the curry leaves and allow to splutter a little.

Add the onions and sauté for 5 minutes, then add salt to taste and stir in the turmeric powder, whole Kashmiri chillies, white wine vinegar and jaggery. Continue to cook the onions until they are a light golden-brown colour.

Add the contents of the pestle and mortar, fresh tomatoes, garlic, ginger, green chillies, grated mango (or tamarind paste) and sundried tomato paste. Stir and continue to cook until you have something that resembles a paste. The pan should become quite dry and the moisture from the onions and tomatoes should have all absorbed.

Now you can stir in the coconut milk, water and the warming spices.

Bring the coconut milk to the boil, immediately reduce to a simmer and allow the coconut milk to thicken for about 8-10 minutes.

Add in the fish, coating it with the sauce and continue to simmer until the fish is cooked. This should take 6-7 minutes. Try not to stir the fish, rather gently shake the pan a little.

Check that the fish is cooked all the way through, remove from the heat, then add the chopped coriander and lime juice and zest.

Stir gently and serve with plain boiled rice.

This is one of the best fish curries which my Dad taught me to cook. It requires raw green mango which most Indian greengrocers sell.

Indian Spicy Haddock Scotch Eggs

Preparation time 30 minutes, cooking time 120 minutes (includes 30 minutes refrigeration)

SERVES 4

250 g haddock (or any white fish)

KEY SPICES
1 tsp black peppercorns
1 1 inch piece of cassia bark
1 Indian bay leaf

½ tsp cumin seeds
½ tsp brown mustard seeds

1 tsp red chilli flakes
¼ tsp turmeric powder

WARMING SPICES
1 tsp fennel seeds
1 tsp fenugreek leaves
¼ tsp nigella seeds

OTHER SPICES
1 tsp mango powder

WET INGREDIENTS
150 g potatoes
4 small fresh eggs
500 ml milk
1 tbs unsalted butter
1 tsp pulped garlic
½ tsp pulped ginger
1 whole green chilli, minced (I have not removed the seeds or membrane, but feel free to if you want a lesser chilli hit)
3 spring onions, finely chopped
1 tsp sundried tomato paste
Zest of half a lime
Handful of fresh coriander, chopped finely

2 fresh eggs, beaten
5 tbs plain flour
5 slices of wholemeal bread, blended to breadcrumbs

Vegetable oil for deep frying

Sea salt to taste

Place the potatoes in a hot oven and bake until tender. Remove and allow to cool. Once cool, scoop the potato out of its skin and place in a bowl.

Boil the 4 eggs in a pan of hot water for 4 minutes. Drain and place them in a bowl of ice cold water to stop the cooking process.

Once cooled, peel the eggs carefully and set aside.

Add the milk to a saucepan, bring to the boil and immediately reduce to a simmer.

Add the black peppercorns, cassia bark, bay leaf and a pinch of sea salt. Allow to simmer for 5 minutes. Add the fish and poach for 5 minutes.

Remove the fish with a slotted spoon and allow to cool.

Heat a small dry frying pan, add the cumin seeds, brown mustard seeds, fennel seeds, fenugreek leaves and nigella seeds. Gently warm through for 1 minute.

Remove from the heat, add to the pestle and mortar, and grind to a powder.

Add the contents of the pestle and mortar to the potatoes. Mix well.

Using the same small frying pan, add the butter on a low heat and allow to melt.

Add the garlic, ginger, green chilli, spring onions, sundried tomato paste, turmeric and chilli flakes. Sauté for 2 minutes.

Remove from the heat and add to the potatoes.

Flake in the fish, and add mango powder, lime zest and chopped coriander. Mix well. Add sea salt to taste.

Place a large spoonful of the mixture in the centre of a piece of cling film, and press out with your hands.

Place an egg in the centre of the mixture and use the cling film to wrap, coat and shape into a ball. Repeat the process with all 4 eggs. Then chill the eggs in the fridge for at least 30 minutes.

Beat two eggs and place in a bowl.

Place the breadcrumbs and flour into separate large shallow bowls.

Roll each egg first into the flour, then the beaten egg, and finally coat with the breadcrumbs.

Once all 4 eggs have been coated, heat the vegetable oil, (add a little piece of bread to ensure the oil is hot - if the bread sizzles, you are ready to fry the spicy haddock scotch eggs).

Carefully add the eggs into the oil, fry until golden brown, turning gently during frying.

Haddock with Coconut Milk and Tamarind

Preparation time 30 minutes,
cooking time 35-40 minutes

SERVES 4

400 g Haddock Fillets, skin removed and
cut into large chunks

KEY SPICES
1 tsp turmeric powder
1 tsp cumin seeds
½ tsp crushed coriander seeds
1 tsp brown mustard seeds
¼ tsp crushed black peppercorns
1 tsp red chilli flakes

WARMING SPICES
1 tsp fenugreek leaves, soaked in 2 tbs hot
water

WET INGREDIENTS
4 tsp tamarind pulp
4 tbs coconut oil
2 banana shallots, finely chopped
200 g good quality chopped tinned
tomatoes
1 tsp pulped garlic
1 tsp pulped ginger
1 fresh bird's eye chilli, pierced
2 tbs fresh grated coconut (frozen will be fine)
200 g coconut milk

Salt flakes or rock salt to taste
10 fresh curry leaves
Small bunch of coriander, roughly chopped
including the stalks

Place the fish in a large bowl and sprinkle with a little salt, then add ½ tsp turmeric powder and 1 tsp of tamarind pulp, ensuring that all the fish has been coated.

Place 2 tbs of the oil in a frying pan, over a high heat.

Gently add the chunks of haddock, sauté for 2-3 minutes or until crisp golden-brown.

Remove the haddock from the pan using a slotted spoon. Set aside to drain on kitchen paper.

Heat a small dry frying pan on a low heat, add the cumin seeds, coriander seeds, brown mustard seeds and black peppercorns. Then warm through for 1 minute, remove from the heat, add to a pestle and mortar and grind to a powder. Set aside.

Heat the remaining oil in a large sauté pan, add the shallots and sauté for 2 minutes.

Add ½ tsp turmeric powder and the red chilli flakes, and continue to sauté for 3 minutes.

Add the curry leaves and continue to sauté for 3 minutes.

Add the contents of the pestle and mortar, tomatoes, garlic, ginger and chilli, and continue to sauté until you see that the mixture resembles a paste.

If the paste becomes a little dry and sticks to the pan, then just add a little water whenever you need, to help you achieve the required consistency.

Add the soaked fenugreek, grated coconut, 3 tsp of tamarind pulp and salt to taste, and continue to cook for a further 2-3 minutes.

Add the coconut milk and bring the mixture to the boil, then immediately reduce to a simmer until the sauce thickens.

Add the haddock chunks, and scoop the sauce on top.

Place a lid on the pan and cook until the fish is heated all the way through.

Remove from the heat, add the fresh coriander, and serve with rice.

This recipe works well with any firm fish. Feel free to swap the bird's eye chilli for a milder one if you prefer. To make it even healthier, you can use light coconut milk.

Mackerel and Gooseberries

Preparation time 20 minutes, cooking time 20 minutes.

SERVES 4

4 fresh mackerel

When cooking mackerel, the secret is only to buy it when it's really fresh. Look for a nice stiff fish with bright eyes.

KEY SPICES
1 tsp cumin seeds
½ tsp crushed coriander seeds
¼ tsp brown mustard seeds
1 1 inch piece of cassia bark
1 Indian bay leaf
¼ tsp turmeric powder
1 tsp red chilli flakes

WARMING SPICES
1 tsp fenugreek leaves, soaked in 2 tbs of hot water

WET INGREDIENTS
1 tbs coconut oil
1 tsp pulped garlic
1 tsp pulped ginger
1 fresh green chilli, pierced
10 pulped gooseberries (you can do this in a blender, or in a pestle and mortar)
2 tbs coconut milk
140 ml water

6 fresh curry leaves
Salt flakes to taste

GARNISH
1 small bunch of fresh coriander, roughly chopped
1 tbs fresh lemon juice
Zest of half a lemon

Heat the oil in a frying pan on a low heat.

Add the key spices and curry leaves, and fry until fragrant. This should take about 1 minute.

Add the garlic, ginger and green chilli, and fry for 1 minute.

Add the pulped gooseberries, coconut milk, water and fenugreek leaves, and simmer on a low heat for 5 minutes.

Add the mackerel, and immediately scoop the mixture in the pan over the mackerel.

Place a lid on the pan for 10 minutes.

Check that the fish is cooked through. The sauce should have infused into the fish and you should be left with a dry fish curry.

Remove from the heat, add fresh coriander, lemon juice and lemon zest and serve immediately.

Mackerel has the reputation of being an acquired taste. I wasn't looking forward to this dish on the first occasion that my Dad made it. I should have known better, my Dad was a culinary genius and knew exactly what to do with this fish. Mackerel is a really good source of vitamin D and some B vitamins, protein and selenium. It's also a rich in omega-3 fatty acids.

Mussels with Green Mango and Coconut Milk

Preparation time 20 minutes, cooking time 30 minutes

SERVES 4

2 lbs mussels, cleaned and beards removed

KEY SPICES
1 tsp cumin seeds
1 tsp crushed coriander seeds
1 tsp brown mustard seeds
1 tsp red chilli flakes
½ tsp turmeric powder

WET INGREDIENTS
2 tbs coconut oil
2 banana shallots, chopped finely
2 tsp pulped garlic
2 tsp pulped ginger
2 mild red chillies, finely sliced
1 tsp sundried tomato paste
1 small green mango, grated finely
2 tsp tamarind pulp
400 ml coconut milk
550 ml water

Sea salt to taste
1 tsp grated jaggery

GARNISH
One small bunch of fresh coriander including stalks, chopped

Heat the oil in large sauté pan over a low heat.

Add the shallots and sea salt to taste, then sauté for 5 minutes.

Add the key spices, and sauté for a further 2 minutes.

Add the garlic, ginger, red chillies, sundried tomato paste and jaggery. Continue stirring for 1 minute.

Add the mango and tamarind pulp, and sauté for 2 minutes.

Add the coconut milk, and water. Stir well, and bring to the boil.

Reduce to a simmer, place the lid on the pan, and cook for 20 minutes.

Increase the heat to medium, add the mussels, cook for 1 minute, then reduce to a simmer and cook for another 5 minutes, or until the mussels have opened up.

Discard any mussels that don't open.

Add the fresh coriander including stalks, and serve immediately.

This is definitely a dish to make when you're entertaining guests. I have used green mango to give a really tangy finish. A relatively easy dish to prepare, brown mustard seeds lend themselves really well to this dish.

Griddled Jumbo Prawns

Preparation time 2 hours and 15 minutes (includes 2 hours refrigeration), cooking time 10 minutes

SERVES 4

20 large jumbo shelled prawns - if you have a fishmonger, ask for them to be deveined.

KEY SPICES
1 tsp cumin seeds

WARMING SPICES
1 tsp fennel seeds

WET INGREDIENTS
2 tbs freshly grated coconut (frozen is fine)
2 tsp pulped garlic
3 tbs dry white wine
3 mild fresh red chillies, chopped or minced finely
2 tbs raw green mango, grated
4 oz unsalted butter, melted

Sea salt to taste

GARNISH
Small bunch of fresh coriander, chopped
Juice and zest of one small lime
Cracked white pepper to taste

Place a small frying pan on a low heat, then add the cumin seeds and fennel seeds and warm for 1 minute

Remove from the heat, place in a pestle and mortar and grind to a powder. Set aside.

In the same pan, on a low heat, add the coconut and toast gently for about 5 minutes until a light golden colour.

Remove from the heat and place in a large bowl along with the ground spices, garlic, white wine, red chillies, mango and butter.

Mix and stir really well, then add the prawns and coat with all the ingredients. Cover and leave in the fridge for 2 hours.

Remove from the fridge and allow the prawns to come up to room temperature.

Place a griddle pan on a high heat and once the pan is really hot, add the prawns. You will probably need to do this in 2 batches.

The prawns should sizzle immediately and begin to turn pink. As they do, turn each prawn over. Once they are fully bright pink, the prawns are cooked.

It is very important not to overcook the prawns. Providing your pan is hot enough, you should only need to cook for 1 minute on each side.

Place the prawns in a large serving dish, stir in the coriander, lime juice and zest, sea salt and cracked white pepper.

Serve immediately.

Dad used to say prawns demand respect Anjula. They are expensive and should be seen as a treat for special occasions. Prawns should be treated with extra care, they need only a little spice and should be cooked briefly'. Sometimes less is more.

Prawns and Coriander

Preparation time 20 minutes, cooking time 25 minutes

You are going to love this recipe. The flavours are incredible, and it only takes a short time to make.

SERVES 4-6

1.5 kg king prawns, deveined with the tails left on
Lay the prawns out on some kitchen paper so that most of the moisture is absorbed. You will get a much tastier dish if the prawns don't contain too much water.

KEY SPICES
1 tsp cumin seeds
1 tsp brown mustard seeds

½ tsp turmeric powder
1 tsp red chilli flakes

WARMING SPICES
1 tsp fennel seeds
1 tsp fenugreek leaves
½ tsp nigella seeds
3 green cardamoms, lightly bashed

OTHER SPICES
¼ tsp ajwain seeds
1 tsp mango powder

WET INGREDIENTS
2 tsp pulped garlic
1 tsp pulped ginger
2 mild fresh red chillies, pierced
Small bunch of fresh coriander including stalks, chopped
Small bunch of fresh mint, chopped
1 tsp sesame oil
1 tbs white wine vinegar
2 tbs vegetable oil
1 large onion, thinly sliced

Sea salt to taste
1 tsp grated jaggery

GARNISH
Juice of one small lime
Zest of one small lime

Warm a large sauté pan on a low heat, add the cumin seeds, mustard seeds, warming spices and ajwain seeds and gently warm through for 1 minute. Remove from the heat.

Discard the husks of the green cardamoms, and add the cardamom seeds, roasted spices, turmeric powder, red chilli flakes, garlic, ginger, red chillies, fresh coriander, fresh mint, sesame oil, and white wine vinegar to a grinder.

Grind until you have a smooth well-blended paste. Set aside.

Add the vegetable oil to the sauté pan which you roasted the spices in, and warm on a low heat.

Add the onion and gently sauté for 5 minutes.

Turn the heat to medium, add salt to taste, and allow the onions to go slightly golden in colour.

Reduce the heat back to a low simmer. Add the paste which you created earlier, as well as the mango powder and jaggery. Stir and cook for 1 minute.

Stir in the prawns, and cook for 5 minutes or until the prawns turn pink

Remove from the heat, add the lime juice and zest, and stir.

Serve with plain boiled rice.

This is a relatively simple dish with amazing flavours. Many people remark that prawns can be very easy to overcook. If you are using frozen prawns, I would recommend that you defrost them overnight in the fridge. I love the texture of king prawns and they hold the flavour of the spices so well.

Goan Prawn Curry

Preparation time 20 minutes,
cooking time 30 minutes

SERVES 4

500 g large tiger prawns, deveined with the
tails left on

KEY SPICES
2 tsp coriander seeds
1 tsp cumin seeds
1 tsp brown mustard seeds
½ tsp black peppercorns

1 Indian bay leaf
1 1 inch piece of cassia bark
1-2 tsp red chilli flakes
½ tsp turmeric powder

WARMING SPICES
1 tsp fennel seeds
1 tsp fenugreek leaves soaked in 2tbs of
hot water

WET INGREDIENTS
1 tbs coconut oil
1 large onion, finely diced
2 large ripe tomatoes, finely chopped
2 tsp pulped garlic
2 tsp pulped ginger
2-4 fresh red chillies, pierced (add less for a
milder curry)
100 g fresh grated coconut (frozen is fine)
100 ml coconut milk
5 tbs water

6-8 fresh curry leaves
1 tbs tamarind pulp

1 tsp grated jaggery
Rock salt or sea salt to taste

FOR THE GARNISH
Small bunch fresh coriander, chopped
roughly
Zest of one small lime
1 tsp fresh lime juice

Place the coriander seeds, cumin seeds, brown mustard seeds and black peppercorns in a small dry frying pan on a low heat, and warm through for 1 minute until fragrant. Place in a pestle and mortar, and grind to a powder. Set aside.

Heat the oil in large frying pan over a low heat, then add the onions, Indian bay leaf, cassia bark, red chilli flakes and turmeric, and gently cook until the onions are golden-brown.

Add the tomatoes, jaggery and the contents of the pestle and mortar, and cook for 2 minutes, stirring occasionally.

Stir in the garlic, ginger and red chillies, and cook for 5 minutes.

Add the grated coconut, and cook for 1 minute.

Take a small dry frying pan and warm the fennel seeds on a low heat for one minute, and crush coarsely in the pestle and mortar. Add the coconut milk, ground fennel seeds, fenugreek and 5 tbs water, and bring to the boil.

Reduce to a simmer for 2 minutes, or until you have a good sauce consistency.

Add the prawns, and simmer for 5 minutes.

Add the curry leaves, tamarind pulp and salt to taste. Cook for a further 2 minutes.

Remove from the heat, add fresh coriander, lime zest and lime juice, then stir.

Serve with steamed basmati rice

I think that this is a delicious, rich and sophisticated dish. It has an explosion of wonderful flavours, with tamarind added for a beautiful balance of sourness. If you can't get hold of tamarind, just add a little good quality vinegar.

Prawns and Mahi Mahi

Preparation time 2 hours and 15 minutes
(includes 2 hours marinating time),
cooking time 40 minutes

Serves 4-6

850g firm white fish (mahi mahi), cut into
large chunks
10 large prawns, peeled and deveined

For the Marinade
½ tsp sea salt flakes
¼ tsp turmeric powder
1 tsp coconut oil
1 tsp pulped garlic
1 tsp pulped ginger
2 tbs fresh lemon juice
1 tbs coriander stalks
2 tbs grated fresh coconut (frozen is fine)
2 tbs tamarind pulp

Key Spices
½ tsp cumin seeds
1 tsp crushed coriander seeds
1 tsp brown mustard seeds

½ tsp turmeric powder
1 tsp red chilli flakes

Warming Spices
1 tsp fenugreek leaves, soaked in 2 tbs hot
water

Other Spices
½ tsp ajwain seeds

Wet Ingredients
2 tbs coconut oil
2 banana shallots, finely diced
2 large fresh tomatoes, finely chopped
1 tsp pulped garlic
1 tsp pulped ginger
3 mild fresh red chillies, pierced
200 ml coconut milk
¼ pint hot water (from the kettle)

Other Ingredients
Sea salt flakes to taste
1 tsp grated jaggery
8 fresh curry leaves
2 tbs tamarind pulp
1 small bunch of coriander, chopped roughly
Zest of one lemon

Place the mahi mahi and the prawns in a large bowl.

Place the marinade ingredients into a pestle and mortar or small blender, and grind to create a paste. Add the paste to the bowl and stir well, ensuring that the mahi mahi and prawns are coated.

Cover the bowl with cling film and place in the fridge for at least two hours.

Remove the bowl from the fridge, and bring to room temperature.

To create the sauce, heat a small dry frying pan on a low heat, add the cumin seeds, coriander seeds, brown mustard seeds and ajwain seeds, and warm through gently for 1 minute.

Remove and add to the pestle and mortar, grind to a powder and set aside.

Heat the coconut oil in a large sauté pan over a low heat, add the shallots and sauté for 1 minute.

Add the turmeric, chilli flakes and salt to taste and sauté for 1 minute.
Add the tomatoes, garlic, ginger, chillies, jaggery, and the contents of the pestle and mortar. Cook on a low heat for about 10 minutes, until you see that the mixture resembles a paste.

If the paste becomes a little dry and sticks to the pan, then just add a little water whenever you need, to help you achieve the required consistency.
Add the coconut milk, stir well then add the hot water, bring to the boil and immediately reduce to a low simmer.

Add the soaked fenugreek, curry leaves and tamarind pulp, and cook for 10 minutes.

Add just the mahi mahi chunks to the sauce, spoon the sauce over the fish, and cook for 5 minutes.

Place the prawns on top of the fish, and put the lid on the pan.

Once the prawns have changed colour, remove from the heat, leaving the lid on the pan for 10 minutes.

Add the fresh coriander and lemon zest, and serve with boiled rice.

'Mahi' in Hawaiian means 'strong'. It's a really easy fish to cook, with a firm texture and pink flesh, but you can substitute your favourite firm fish.

Salmon Wrapped in Banana Leaves

Preparation time 2 hours and 20 minutes (includes 2 hours marinating in the fridge), cooking time 20 minutes

SERVES 4

4 thick salmon fillets, skin removed
4 banana leaves, each big enough to wrap a fillet in

KEY SPICES
1 tsp cumin seeds
1 tsp coriander seeds
¼ tsp black peppercorns

WARMING SPICES
1 tsp fennel seeds

OTHER SPICES
2 tsp mango powder

WET INGREDIENTS
100 ml coconut milk
1 tbs white wine vinegar
2 tsp pulped garlic
1 tsp pulped ginger
2 birds eye red chillies, de-seeded and chopped
4 sprigs of spring onions
6-8 fresh curry leaves snipped into tiny pieces with a scissors (optional)
2 tbs coconut oil (plus a little extra for brushing)
Stalks from a small bunch of fresh coriander, finely chopped

Sea salt to taste
2 tsp jaggery

GARNISH
1 small bunch of coriander chopped
Juice and zest of a small lime

Except for the garnish ingredients, salmon and banana leaves, place all the ingredients in a grinder and blend to a paste. Remove and place in a large bowl.

Add the salmon fillets to the bowl and coat with the marinade. Place cling film over the bowl and place in the fridge for at least 2 hours.

Remove from the fridge and allow the fish to come to room temperature for about 15 minutes.

Pre-heat the oven to 200°C, 400°F or gas mark 6.

Soak the banana leaves in hot water for a few minutes to make them pliable, then remove from the water and dry them gently with kitchen paper.

Take a pastry brush and paint a thin layer of coconut oil all over each banana leaf.

Place each fillet in the middle of the banana leaf, top with some of the paste and create a parcel, secured with cocktail sticks.

If I am entertaining, I buy really long chives and take a few together and tie the parcel with these. It looks a little bit more special.

Place the parcels on a baking tray and bake for 15 minutes. Remove from the oven.

Mix together the coriander leaves, lime zest and juice, and place in a small bowl.

Take the parcels to the table and allow your guest to open them. Pass around the garnish to each guest to add to the salmon.

Serve with warm chapattis.

If it is difficult for you to find banana leaves, you can use baking paper or foil. Most Indian greengrocers or Asian shops sell frozen banana leaves. You can also use any firm fish of your choice as an alternative.

Growing up, we had the most amazing fishmongers in Southall Broadway. We called the owner 'Roe' and only found out years later that this was not his real name - he was always joking with us. Dad was always helping 'Roe' with his troublesome van and first discovered salmon when 'Roe' gave him a whole salmon for fixing his van. This is a great entertaining dish, which is so easy that you could almost make it with your eyes closed.

Grilled Halibut
with Stir Fried Vegetables

Preparation time 30 minutes, cooking time 2 hours and 40 minutes (which includes 2 hours refrigeration)

SERVES 4

4 halibut steaks

KEY SPICES
1 tsp cumin seeds
½ tsp brown mustard seeds

½ tsp turmeric powder
1 tsp red chilli flakes

WARMING SPICES
1 tsp fennel seeds
1 tsp fenugreek leaves

OTHER SPICES
1 heaped tsp mango powder

WET INGREDIENTS
1 tsp white wine vinegar
1 tbs sundried tomato paste
1 tsp pulped garlic
1 tsp pulped ginger
1 green chilli, sliced lengthways
1 courgette, cut into strips
1 red pepper, de-seeded and cut into strips
1 green pepper, de-seeded and cut into strips
3 spring onions, finely chopped
2 tbs butter, melted
1 tbs groundnut oil or vegetable oil

Salt flakes to taste

GARNISH
Zest of one small lime
Juice of one small lime
Small bunch of fresh coriander with stalks, chopped

Place a dry pan on a low heat, add the cumin seeds, brown mustard seeds and warming spices. Gently warm through for 1 minute.

Remove from the heat, place the roasted spices in a pestle and mortar, add the turmeric powder and red chilli flakes and grind to a powder. Add salt to taste.

Place the contents of the pestle and mortar in a large bowl along with the white wine vinegar, sundried tomato paste, garlic, ginger and green chilli.

Stir well, add the halibut and coat well with the spices.

Add the courgettes, red and green peppers, spring onions and mango powder. Stir well.

Cover with cling film, and refrigerate for at least two hours.

Remove from the fridge, and allow the halibut to come up to room temperature.

Remove the halibut steaks from the bowl, brush them with melted butter on both sides, and place under a grill on a medium heat for about 3-5 minutes on each side, or until cooked through.

Meanwhile heat the oil in a wok or frying pan, add the remaining contents of the large bowl and fry the vegetables on a high heat for 2 minutes. Remove from the heat.

Mix together the lime zest, lime juice and coriander to create the garnish.

Take half of the garnish and stir it into the vegetables, and brush the other half onto the halibut steaks. Serve immediately.

This is an exceptionally healthy dish, which can be made even healthier by replacing the butter with a little additional groundnut oil. Halibut is the largest of all flat fish, occasionally growing to two metres or more in length. I think it is firm and incredibly tasty, but it can dry out easily so needs to be cooked carefully.

VEGETARIAN

This is the colander which I used as a little girl. I used it to collect whatever Dad sent me to the back garden to pick. It's very old and full of nostalgia and memories.

Burnt Aubergine
and Dry Pomegranate Seeds

Preparation time 30 minutes,
cooking time 60 minutes

SERVES 4-6

4 aubergines, medium size

KEY SPICES
1 tsp cumin seeds
1 tsp coriander seeds
1 tsp brown mustard seeds
½ tsp black peppercorns

1 1 inch piece of cassia bark
1 Indian bay leaf

1 tsp turmeric powder
1 tsp red chilli flakes

WARMING SPICES
1 tsp fennel seeds
6 green cardamoms, lightly bashed

WET INGREDIENTS
4 tbs vegetable oil
1 large onion, finely chopped
4 fresh beef tomatoes, roughly chopped
1 tbs tomato puree
2 tsp pulped garlic
2 tsp pulped ginger
2-3 green chillies, pierced
4 tbs water

OTHER INGREDIENTS
2 tbs pomegranate seeds
8 fresh curry leaves
1 tsp grated jaggery
6 whole dry Kashmiri chillies

Small bunch of fresh coriander, roughly chopped

Sea or rock salt

Soak the pomegranate seeds in 3 tbs of hot water for 10 minutes. Grind in the pestle and mortar, creating a fine paste. Set aside.

Wash the aubergines and dry thoroughly with kitchen paper. Using tongs, place each aubergine directly over the flames on a gas hob, turning as the aubergine starts to burn all over and the flesh becomes soft. If you do not have a gas hob you can put the aubergines under a grill, which takes a little longer.

Allow the aubergines to cool and then mash them coarsely. Set aside.

Take a small dry frying pan, set on a low heat, and warm through the cumin seeds, coriander seeds, brown mustard seeds and black peppercorns until fragrant. This should take 1 minute, as you are just trying to tease the oil out of the spices. Remove from the heat, add to the pestle and mortar and grind coarsely.

Take a large sauté pan, add the oil and warm on a low heat. Then add the onion, cassia bark, Indian bay leaf and salt to taste. Sauté for 5 minutes.

Add the turmeric powder and red chilli flakes, stir and sauté for 2 minutes.

Add the aubergines, beef tomatoes, tomato puree, jaggery, pomegranate paste and curry leaves and sauté for a further 10 minutes, stirring occasionally.

By cooking these ingredients for a little longer, your curry will definitely taste better.

Now add the Kashmiri chillies, garlic, ginger and green chillies, and sauté for 2 minutes.

Add the contents of the pestle and mortar, stir well, and sauté for about 10 minutes, until you see that the mixture resembles a paste.

If the paste becomes a little dry and sticks to the pan, then just add a little water whenever you need, to help you achieve the required consistency.

In a dry frying pan, roast the warming spices for 1 minute until fragrant, and add to the large sauté pan.

Stir well and add 4 tbs water. Bring to a simmer, place lid on the pan and cook for 25 minutes.

Switch off the heat, add the fresh coriander. Serve with fresh chapattis.

Remember to count your cardamoms in and count them out again before serving.

Cabbage and Carrot Thoran

Preparation time 20 minutes, cooking time 25 minutes

SERVES 3-4

1 medium sized cabbage, shredded coarsely with a hand grater
3 large carrots, shredded coarsely with a hand grater

KEY SPICES
1 tsp cumin seeds
1 tsp brown mustard seeds
½ tsp turmeric powder
1 tsp red chilli flakes

WARMING SPICES
1 tsp fennel seeds
1 tsp fenugreek leaves, soaked in 2 tbs of hot water

OTHER SPICES
½ tsp asafoetida

WET INGREDIENTS
2 tbs coconut oil
4-5 shallots, finely chopped
1-2 green chillies, slit lengthways
50 g grated coconut, fresh or frozen

10 fresh curry leaves
Salt flakes to taste
Small bunch of fresh coriander, roughly chopped

Heat the coconut oil in a large frying pan or wok.

Add the asafoetida and the key spices and sauté until fragrant. This should take 1 minute.

Add the shallots and sauté until translucent.

Add the green chilli(es), warming spices and curry leaves, and sauté for 1 minute.

Add the cabbage, carrots and salt. Stir and sauté for 1 minute, then place the lid on the pan, and cook for 10 minutes stirring occasionally.

Add the coconut, stir and cook for 2-3 minutes without the lid on, until the moisture is absorbed.

Add the fresh coriander, and serve immediately.

Thoran is a dry curry from Kerala, made from fresh vegetables. You can also make this dish with lemon grass. Simply replace the curry leaves with two stalks of lemon grass. Give the lemon grass a really good bash, add it in along with the shallots and then remove before serving.

Roasted Aubergines with Fresh Coconut

Preparation time 20 minutes, cooking time 45 minutes (includes 30 minutes marinating)

SERVES 4

8 small slim aubergines
2 tbs freshly grated coconut (frozen is fine)

KEY SPICES
½ tsp turmeric powder
1 tsp red chilli flakes
1 tsp cumin seeds
½ tsp brown mustard seeds

WARMING SPICES
1 tsp fenugreek leaves
1 tsp fennel seeds

OTHER SPICES
1 tsp mango powder

WET INGREDIENTS
Juice of 1 whole lime
200 ml natural plain yogurt
8 fresh curry leaves, ripped into small pieces (optional)
1 tbs coconut oil
2 tsp pulped garlic
1 tsp pulped ginger
1 tsp sundried tomato paste
1 fresh green chilli, minced

Sprinkle of sea salt
1 tsp grated jaggery

GARNISH
Small bunch of coriander including stalks chopped finely
Zest of one whole lime

Butterfly the aubergines in half lengthways, opening them like a book, and then gently flatten.

Score the surfaces with a criss-cross pattern, place in a large bowl, squeeze the lime juice over them, then sprinkle a little sea salt, add the natural yogurt, curry leaves, turmeric powder and red chilli flakes and ensure you coat the aubergines well. Set aside.

Take a small dry pan and set on a low heat, add the cumin seeds and brown mustard seeds and the warming spices.

Gently warm through for 1 minute, remove from the heat, place in a pestle and mortar, and grind to a powder.

Add the contents of the pestle and mortar to the aubergines along with the coconut oil, garlic, ginger, sundried tomato paste, green chilli, mango powder and jaggery. Mix thoroughly, cover and leave in a cool place to marinate for 30 minutes.

Meanwhile toast the fresh coconut on a low heat until light golden-brown. Set aside to cool.

You can either cook the aubergines on hot coals outdoors or under a hot grill for just 3 minutes on either side. Remove from the heat, mix together the lime zest, toasted coconut and fresh coriander and sprinkle over the top of the aubergines.

Serve with fresh chapattis, and a chutney of your choice.

Aubergines are a hit or miss for many people. If you pair them with the right spices and sprinkle with a little salt to help remove some of the bitterness, aubergines come into their own. It is technically a fruit, but is used as a vegetable. It's grown all over the world, and comes in many different varieties. Rich in antioxidants, aubergines are an excellent source of dietary fibre. They also contain vitamins B1 and B6 as well as potassium, magnesium and copper.

Cauliflower Kofta

Preparation time 40 minutes,
cooking time 45 minutes

SERVES 6

1 large cauliflower, rinsed and grated. Then laid out on a clean tea towel to absorb the water. Use the inner lighter green leaves too, which have lots of flavour.

FOR THE KOFTA
1 tsp cumin seeds
1 tsp coriander seeds
1 medium sized potato, boiled or baked in the oven. I prefer to bake.
1 tsp red chilli flakes
1 tsp fenugreek leaves
1 tsp mango powder
Stalks of one small bunch of coriander, chopped finely
1 tsp pulped ginger
2 tbs corn flour
¼ tsp baking powder
1 tsp sunflower oil
Sea salt to taste

Vegetable oil to deep fry the kofta

FOR THE BROTH
Key Spices
1 tsp cumin seeds
1 tsp brown mustard seeds
1 1 inch piece of cassia bark
1 Indian bay leaf

1 tsp turmeric powder
1 tsp red chilli flakes

WARMING SPICES
1 tsp fennel seeds
2 cloves

WET INGREDIENTS
2 tbs sunflower oil
1 medium sized onion, chopped finely
2 tbs sundried tomato paste
2 tsp pulped garlic
2 fresh green chillies, pierced
280 ml water
2 tbs thick natural yogurt

1 tsp grated jaggery
Sea salt to taste

GARNISH
1 small bunch of fresh coriander leaves, chopped roughly
Zest and juice of one small lime

Place a small dry sauté pan on a low heat and once warm, heat the cumin seeds and the coriander seeds for 1 minute. Remove from the heat and place in a pestle and mortar. Grind coarsely and set aside.

Place a large sauté pan on a low heat, add the grated cauliflower and sauté for 5-7 minutes.

Remove from the heat and transfer to a large bowl.

Scoop out the contents of the baked potato and add to the bowl.

Add the contents of the pestle and mortar and all the remaining kofta ingredients to the bowl.

Mix and add sea salt to taste.

Using clean hands to mix and blend all of the spices, you should find everything comes together and you will be able to form small golf ball sized kofta. If you find that the mixture is not holding, then just add a little more corn flour.

Heat some oil to deep fry the kofta. Once the oil is hot, fry the kofta until a light golden-brown colour, for about 2 - 3 minutes. Drain the kofta and place on absorbent kitchen paper.

To make the broth, place a sauté pan on a low heat, add the oil and once warm add the cumin seeds, brown mustard seeds, cassia bark and Indian bay leaf. Allow to warm through for 1 minute.

Add the onion and sauté until a light golden-brown colour.

Add the turmeric powder, red chilli flakes, sundried tomato paste, garlic, green chillies, and jaggery. Continue to sauté for 5 minutes.

Whisk the water and yogurt together, add to the pan bring to a boil and then immediately reduce to a gentle simmer.

Add the warming spices, simmer for 5 minutes and add sea salt to taste.

Remove from the heat, add the fresh coriander leaves, lime juice and zest, and stir. Remember to count out the cloves.

Place the fried kofta in the broth and place a lid on the pan. Allow the kofta to sit in the broth for 5 minutes before serving.

Serve with chapattis (my preference) or rice.

If you don't like cauliflower, this is a dish which hopefully will change your mind.

Cauliflower, Carrot, Mangetout and Red Pepper Indian Stir Fry

Preparation time 30 minutes,
cooking time 30 minutes

SERVES 4

KEY SPICES
1 tsp cumin seeds
1 tsp brown mustard seeds

½ tsp turmeric powder
1 tsp red chilli flakes

WARMING SPICES
¼ tsp nigella seeds
½ tsp fennel seeds
1 tsp fenugreek leaves

OTHER SPICES
2 tsp asafoetida

WET INGREDIENTS
1 small cauliflower, cut into bite size florets
2 medium size carrots, sliced thinly
3 tbs coconut oil
1 tsp pulped garlic
1 tsp pulped ginger
2 large fresh ripe tomatoes, chopped finely
115 g mangetout
1 red pepper, sliced into thin strips
1 tbs tamarind pulp

6 fresh curry leaves
1 tsp grated jaggery
Himalayan pink rock salt to taste
Small bunch of coriander, roughly chopped

Bring a pot of water to the boil, then add 1 tsp of asafoetida

Add the cauliflower and carrots, and boil for 2 minutes.

Strain the cauliflower and carrots and run them under a cold water to stop the cooking process.

Drain and set aside.

Place a small dry frying pan on a low heat, add the cumin seeds, brown mustard seeds and warming spices and warm through for 1 minute.

Remove the spices from the pan, pour them into the pestle and mortar, and grind to a powder. Set aside.

In a large sauté pan, heat the coconut oil on a medium heat. Add 1 tsp of asafoetida and the curry leaves, and allow to sizzle.

Add the ginger and garlic, and sauté for 1 minute.

Add the chopped tomatoes, jaggery, the contents of the pestle and mortar, turmeric powder, red chilli flakes and salt to taste. Cook until you see that the mixture resembles a paste. This should take between 5 and 8 minutes.

If the paste becomes a little dry and sticks to the pan, then just add a little water whenever you need, to help you achieve the required consistency.

Add the cauliflower and carrots to the sauté pan, cook for 3 to 4 minutes on a medium heat. If required, sprinkle a little water on during this stage too.

Turn the heat on high and add the mangetout, red peppers and tamarind pulp. Stir well and cook for 1 minute.

Switch off the heat, place the lid on the pan and leave for 10 minutes.

Add the chopped coriander.

Serve with fresh chapattis.

These are fantastically healthy ingredients to combine in a quick curry, after a hard day's work. You can use pretty much any vegetables in the fridge, that's exactly what my Dad and I used to do.

Indian French Fries and Peas

Preparation time 15 minutes, cooking time 30 minutes

SERVES 4

450 g frozen French Fries
50 g frozen peas

KEY SPICES
1 tsp turmeric powder
1 tsp red chilli flakes

1 tsp cumin seeds
1 tsp crushed coriander seeds
1 tsp brown mustard seeds

WARMING SPICES
1 tsp fenugreek seeds, soaked in 2 tbs hot water
1 tsp fennel seeds

OTHER SPICES
1 tsp asafoetida
2 tsp mango powder

WET INGREDIENTS
2 tbs coconut oil
2 tsp pulped garlic
1 tsp pulped ginger
3 medium size fresh tomatoes, puréed
1 tsp sundried tomato paste
4 tbs water

1 tsp jaggery
Small bunch of fresh coriander. Stalks finely chopped, and leaves separately roughly chopped.

Soak the turmeric powder and red chilli flakes in 2 tbs hot kettle water. Set aside.

Heat a small dry pan on a low flame, add the cumin seeds, coriander seeds, mustard seeds and fennel seeds. Stir and warm for 1 minute until fragrant.

Remove the pan from the heat, add the contents to a pestle and mortar, and coarsely grind. Set aside.

Heat the coconut oil in a large sauté pan over a low heat, add the asafoetida and allow to warm through, then add the garlic and ginger, and fry for 30 seconds.

Add the soaked turmeric and chilli flakes and the spices from the pestle and mortar and gently sauté on a low heat for just 30 seconds (be careful not to burn the garlic & ginger).

Add the tomatoes, tomato paste and jaggery, and cook on a low simmer until you see that the mixture resembles a paste.

If the paste becomes a little dry and sticks to the pan, then just add a little water whenever you need, to help you achieve the required consistency.

Add the mango powder and soaked fenugreek, and stir well.

Add the French Fries, and coat with all the spices.

Add 4 tbs of water, and add the chopped coriander stalks.

Reduce to a low simmer, place the lid on the pan and cook for 10 minutes, stirring occasionally.

Add the peas, stir and cook for a further minute without the lid on.

Remove from the heat, add the fresh chopped coriander leaves and serve with chapattis.

This is an improvised and simple recipe, with the key ingredients taken straight from the freezer.

Fine Green Beans with Mango and Tomatoes

Preparation time 15 minutes, cooking time 20 minutes

SERVES 4

KEY SPICES
1 tsp cumin seeds
1 tsp brown mustard seeds

¼ tsp turmeric powder
1 tsp red chilli flakes

WARMING SPICES
1 tsp fennel seeds
1 tsp fenugreek leaves
¼ tsp nigella seeds

OTHER SPICES
¼ tsp asafoetida
¼ tsp sesame seeds
1 tsp mango powder

WET INGREDIENTS
2 tbs coconut oil
1 tsp pulped garlic
1 tsp pulped ginger
450 g fine green beans trimmed, halved and blanched for 1 minute.
2 fresh tomatoes, cut into wedges.
1 large unripened mango, cut into small squares.

Himalayan pink rock salt to taste
Small bunch of fresh coriander, roughly chopped

Place a small dry frying pan on a low heat. Add the cumin seeds, brown mustard seeds and warming spices to the pan and gently warm through for 1 minute.

Pour the contents of the pan into a pestle and mortar, grind to a powder and set aside.

Warm the oil in a large sauté pan on a medium heat, add the asafoetida and sesame seeds.

As soon as the sesame seeds start popping, add the garlic and ginger, and sauté for 1 minute.

Add the turmeric powder, red chilli flakes and the contents of the pestle and mortar. Stir well and cook for 1 minute

Remove the pan from the heat, and stir in the green beans.

Place the pan back on a medium heat. Stir and cook gently for 1 minute.

Add the tomato wedges, mango, mango powder and salt, stirring really well. Cook on a high heat for 1 minute.

Remove from the heat, place the lid on the pan for 10 minutes, and add the fresh coriander.

Serve with warm chapattis.

This recipe is one of my all-time favourites. I always think of it as a great outdoor dish – refreshing and vibrant – it goes well with fish, poultry and red meat.

Ripe Mango Curry

Preparation time 20 minutes, cooking time 20 minutes

Serves 4

KEY SPICES
½ tsp turmeric powder
1 tsp red chilli flakes
1 tsp brown mustard seeds
1 tsp cumin seeds

WARMING SPICES
1 tsp fenugreek leaves
¼ tsp nigella seeds
1 tsp fennel seeds

OTHER SPICES
1 tsp asafoetida

WET INGREDIENTS
3 tbs coconut oil
1 tsp pulped garlic
1 tsp pulped ginger
2 green chillies, pierced
3 tbs water
4 medium sized ripe mangoes, skin removed and cubed
1 tbs fresh coconut (frozen will also be fine)

6 curry leaves, ripped
2 tsp grated jaggery
Small bunch of fresh coriander, roughly chopped
Rock or sea salt to taste

Add the coconut oil to a large sauté pan on a low heat, add the key spices, warming spices and asafoetida. Sauté for 1 minute.

Add the garlic, ginger, green chillies, water, curry leaves and jaggery. Sauté for 3 minutes.

Add the mangoes and coconut, stirring really well.

Add rock salt to taste, and sauté for 5 minutes.

Remove from the heat, place the lid on the pan, and leave for 10 minutes. Add fresh coriander.

This isn't a well-known dish. It's so simple to create, and is a great dish to make if you're busy. Every chef has their favourite ingredients, and mango is definitely one of mine. I have always loved the special and distinctive taste and the fragrance. Mangoes are rich in vitamin C.

Okra with Brown Chickpeas

Preparation 30 minutes,
cooking time 60 minutes

SERVES 4

500 g fresh okra, cut diagonally into 2 cm pieces. You should clean the okra with a damp cloth, rather than washing it under a running tap.
200 g brown chickpeas

KEY SPICES
1 tsp cumin seeds
1 tsp coriander seeds
½ tsp brown mustard seeds
¼ tsp black peppercorns

1 1 inch piece of cassia bark
1 Indian bay leaf

½ tsp turmeric powder
1 tsp red chilli flakes

WARMING SPICES
2 cloves
2 green cardamoms, lightly bashed

OTHER SPICES
1 tsp chana masala

WET INGREDIENTS
2 tbs lemon juice
3 tbs vegetable oil
1 large onion, finely chopped
1 tsp pulped garlic
1 tsp pulped ginger
1-2 fresh green chillies, pierced
3 ripe fresh tomatoes, chopped

1 tsp grated jaggery
Sea salt to taste
Small bunch of fresh coriander, roughly chopped

Place the chopped okra in a small bowl, pour over the lemon juice, stir well, cover and set aside.

Thoroughly rinse the brown chickpeas in cold water and set aside.

Place a small dry frying pan on a low heat, add the cumin seeds, coriander seeds, mustard seeds, black peppercorns and the warming spices. Warm through for 1 minute.

Remove the green cardamom and cloves. Set aside.

Pour the remaining spices from the pan into the pestle and mortar, and grind to a powder. Set aside.

In a large sauté pan, heat the oil on a medium heat, then add the onion, cassia bark and Indian bay leaf, and sauté until the onions are a golden-brown colour, stirring occasionally.

Add the garlic, ginger and green chillies and sauté for 1 minute.

Add the turmeric powder, red chilli flakes, tomatoes, jaggery, salt to taste and the contents of the pestle and mortar. Cook until you see that the mixture resembles a paste. This should between 5 and 8 minutes.

If the paste becomes a little dry and sticks to the pan, then just add a little water whenever you need, to help you achieve the required consistency.

Add the okra, coat well in the spices, turn the heat to high, and sauté for 3 minutes.

Add the chickpeas, cloves and green cardamom, stir well, place the lid on the pan, and cook for 15 minutes on a low simmer.

Remove from the heat, stir in the chana masala and chopped coriander, and then place the lid back on the pan for 5 minutes.

This is to allow the chana masala to infuse the chickpeas and okra.

Serve with fresh chapattis.

Remember to count your cardamoms and cloves in and count them out again before serving.

Okra may be a new vegetable for you to cook, and if so, I encourage you to give it a try. The combination of Okra and Chickpeas is great. Recently Okra has been suggested to help manage blood sugar in cases of type 1 and type 2 diabetes. Okra is also known as ladies' fingers, and is a flowering plant in the mallow family.

Paneer and Peas
with Mango Pickle

Preparation time 20 minutes,
cooking time 55 minutes

SERVES 4

200 g paneer

KEY SPICES
1 Indian bay leaf
1 1 inch piece of cassia bark
1 tsp red chilli flakes
½ tsp turmeric powder

1 tsp cumin seeds
1 tsp coriander seeds
½ tsp brown mustard seeds
¼ tsp black peppercorns

WARMING SPICES
1 tsp fenugreek leaves, soaked in 2 tbs
water

WET INGREDIENTS
2 tbs vegetable oil
1 large onion, finely chopped
300 g good quality chopped tinned
tomatoes
2 tbs mango pickle
2 tsp pulped garlic
1 tsp pulped ginger
2 green chillies, pierced
100 g frozen peas
3 tbs hot water

1 tsp grated jaggery
Rock salt or salt flakes to taste

GARNISH
Juice of half a lemon
Zest of half a fresh lemon
1 small bunch of coriander, roughly
chopped

Soak the paneer whole in hot water for 10 minutes, drain and place on a kitchen towel and allow to cool. Then cut into bite size pieces and set aside.

In a dry frying pan gently warm through the cumin seeds, coriander seeds, brown mustard seeds and black peppercorns, over a low heat for 1 minute until fragrant. Add to a pestle and mortar, and grind coarsely.

Heat 1 tbs of the oil in a large sauté pan, over a medium heat.

Fry the paneer until golden-brown on all sides. Remove from the pan with a slotted spoon, and place on kitchen paper to absorb any excess oil.

Add the remaining oil to the sauté pan,

Add the onion and salt, and cook for 5 minutes, or until the onions are translucent and soft.

Add the Indian bay leaf, cassia bark, red chilli flakes and turmeric powder. Stir well, and sauté for a further 2 minutes. Add the tinned tomatoes, mango pickle and jaggery, stir well, and cook until the oil appears on the surface of the tomatoes. This should take about 10 minutes.

Add the spices from the pestle and mortar, stir really well and cook for 2 minutes.

Add the garlic, ginger and green chillies, and cook for 2 minutes.

Add the fenugreek and fried paneer, and cook for a further 5 minutes.

Add the peas and hot water, place a lid on the pan and cook for a further 3 minutes.

Remove the pan from the heat, add the lemon juice, lemon zest and fresh coriander. Stir well and place the lid back on the pan (but not on the heat) for 5 minutes.

Serve with chapattis.

I love this dish, made with smooth and silky paneer. The paneer has a delicious crisp outer crunch and works well with the sour, zingy mango pickle. I make my own mango pickle, but feel free to buy a good quality mango pickle when you make it.

Black-Eyed Peas
with Roasted Peppers

Preparation time 30 minutes, cooking time 1 hour and 40 minutes. Soak overnight.

SERVES 4

150 g black-eyed peas
4 red peppers, cut into half with stalks remaining, but the seeds and core removed

KEY SPICES
1 tsp cumin seeds
1 tsp crushed coriander seeds
¼ tsp brown mustard seeds

1 Indian bay leaf
1 1 inch piece of cassia bark

1 tsp red chilli flakes
¼ tsp turmeric powder

WARMING SPICES
1 tsp fenugreek, soaked in 2 tbs hot water

OTHER SPICES
¼ tsp asafoetida
½ tsp ajwain seeds
1 tsp mango powder

WET INGREDIENTS
Coconut oil spray
2 tbs coconut oil
2 medium onions, finely chopped
1 tsp pulped garlic
1 tsp pulped ginger
2 fresh green chillies, pierced
2 fresh tomatoes, finely chopped
1 tsp sundried tomato paste

1 tsp grated jaggery
Rock salt or salt flakes to taste

Small bunch of fresh coriander, roughly chopped
4 wedges of fresh lemon

Wash and soak the peas overnight.

Rinse the peas and place in a saucepan.

Add just enough water to cover the peas. Bring to the boil, add the asafoetida, then cover and simmer gently until tender but not mushy, which should take 25-30 minutes.

Drain the peas, but keep the drained water.

Pre-heat the oven to 180 C, 260 F or gas mark 4

Put the peppers into a shallow roasting tin, spray with coconut oil, sprinkle the ajwain seeds evenly over the peppers and roast in the oven for 30 minutes.

Place a small dry frying pan on a low heat add the cumin seeds, coriander seeds and brown mustard seeds and gently warm for 1 minute.

Remove from the heat, add to the pestle and mortar and grind coarsely. Set aside.

In a large sauté pan, heat the coconut oil on a low heat, add the Indian bay leaf, cassia bark and onions and sauté for 2-3 minutes.

Add the garlic, ginger, red chilli flakes, turmeric powder, chillies and salt to taste, and sauté for 1 minute.

Add the tomatoes, sundried tomato paste, jaggery and the contents of the pestle and mortar, and sauté until you see that the mixture resembles a paste. This should between 5 and 8 minutes.

If the paste becomes a little dry and sticks to the pan, then just add a little water whenever you need, to help you achieve the required consistency.

Add the peas to the large sauté pan, mix and stir well. Cook for 10 minutes, adding a little of the drained water if the mixture becomes dry.

NB - The peas should become semi-dry, so that you can scoop them into the half peppers.

Add the fenugreek leaves and mango powder, and cook for 5 minutes.

Remove from the heat, add the fresh coriander leaves, then fill the roasted peppers with the peas. Serve with the lemon wedges, chapattis and a cucumber raita.

Portobello Mushrooms with Roasted Rich Tomatoes

Preparation time 30 minutes, cooking time 80 minutes

SERVES 4

6 portobello mushrooms, stalks removed and cleaned with a damp cloth, each mushroom sliced into 6 even slices
4 large juicy beef tomatoes

KEY SPICES
1 tsp cumin seeds
1 tsp coriander seeds
½ tsp mustard seeds
½ tsp black peppercorns

1 1 inch piece of cassia bark
1 Indian bay leaf

½ tsp turmeric powder
1 tsp red chilli flakes

WARMING SPICES
1 tsp fenugreek leaves, soaked in 2 tbs of hot water
½ tsp fennel seeds
4 green cardamoms, lightly bashed
1 black cardamom, lightly bashed
2 cloves

OTHER SPICES
½ tsp ajwain seeds

WET INGREDIENTS
3 tbs groundnut oil
2 medium size onions, finely chopped
2 tsp pulped garlic
1 tsp pulped ginger
2 green chillies, pierced

1 tsp jaggery
Sea salt or salt flakes to taste
Freshly ground pepper

GARNISH
Small bunch of coriander including stalks, chopped
Juice and zest of one small lime

Pre heat the oven to 180 C (260 F) or gas mark 4

Wash the beef tomatoes and cut into large wedges, transfer to a baking tray, sprinkle on a little salt flakes and freshly ground pepper, and roast in the oven for 15 minutes.

Remove from the oven and set aside.

Take a small dry frying pan, set on a low heat, and warm through the cumin seeds, coriander seeds, brown mustard seeds and black peppercorns until fragrant. This should take 1 minute, as you are just trying to tease the oil out of the spices. Remove from the heat, add to the pestle and mortar and grind coarsely.

In the same small dry frying pan, on a low heat, roast the warming spices and ajwain seeds, (leave out the soaked fenugreek leaves) roasting until fragrant for 1 minute. Set aside.

Take a large sauté pan, add the oil and warm on a low heat. Then add the onions, cassia bark and Indian bay leaf. Sauté for 5 minutes.

Add the turmeric powder and red chilli flakes, stir and sauté for 2 minutes.

Add the roasted beef tomatoes, jaggery and salt to taste, and continue to sauté for a further 10 minutes, stirring occasionally.

By cooking these ingredients for a little longer, your curry will definitely taste better.

Now add the garlic, ginger and green chillies and sauté for 2 minutes.

Add the contents of the pestle and mortar, stir well, and sauté for about 10 minutes, until you see that the mixture resembles a paste.

If the paste becomes a little dry and sticks to the pan, then just add a little water whenever you need, to help you achieve the required consistency.

Add the fenugreek leaves and the roasted warming spices, stir well and cook for 1 minute.

Add the mushrooms, turn the heat to high and cook for 15 minutes. Remember that the mushrooms contain water, hence the reason the heat is turned up high for this particular dish.

Reduce the heat to simmer, chop the coriander stalks up finely and add to the pan.

Stir and place the lid on the pan, cooking for a further 10 minutes.

Remove from the heat, add the chopped fresh coriander leaves, lime juice and zest. Stir well.

Serve with chapattis.

Remember to count your cardamoms and cloves in and count them out again before serving.

Spinach and Chickpeas with Coconut Milk

Preparation time 30 minutes, cooking time 60 minutes

SERVES 4

240 g baby spinach
400 g canned chickpeas
400 ml coconut milk

KEY SPICES
1 tsp cumin seeds
1 tsp brown mustard seeds

1 1 inch piece of cassia bark
1 Indian bay leaf

½ tsp turmeric powder
1 tsp red chilli flakes

WARMING SPICES
4 green cardamoms, lightly bashed
1 tsp fennel seeds
1 tsp fenugreek leaves

WET INGREDIENTS
3 tbs coconut oil
2 medium size onions, finely chopped
2 tsp pulped garlic
1 tsp pulped ginger
1 - 2 green chillies, pierced
6-8 semi-dried tomatoes, minced
1 tsp sundried tomato paste
2 tbs lemon juice
Zest of one small lemon

Sea salt to taste
½ tsp grated jaggery
Small bunch of fresh coriander, roughly chopped

Bring a pot of water to the boil, and drop the spinach leaves into the boiling water.

Allow the spinach to boil for 1 minute, then remove from the heat.
Carefully drain the spinach in a colander, run under a cold tap to stop the cooking process, and then gently shake the colander to remove excess water from the spinach.

Place the spinach into a blender and blitz into a purée. Set aside.

Place a small dry frying pan on a low heat, add the cumin seeds and brown mustard seeds, and warm for 1 minute.

Remove from the heat, place in a pestle and mortar, grind coarsely and set aside.

In the same dry frying pan, on a low heat, warm the warming spices for 1 minute and set aside.

Place a large sauté pan on a low heat, warm the coconut oil and then add the cassia bark, Indian bay leaf, onions and sea salt to taste.

Gently sauté for 5 minutes, add the turmeric powder and red chilli flakes and cook for 1 minute.

Add the garlic, ginger, pierced green chillies, semi-dried tomatoes, sundried tomato paste and jaggery. Stir and cook on a low heat for 10 minutes.

Add the contents of the pestle and mortar and the chickpeas, and cook over a medium heat for a few minutes, or until the chickpeas are beginning to turn golden-brown.

Add the puréed spinach and the roasted warming spices, stir really well and cook on a low heat for 5 minutes.

Add the coconut milk and lemon juice, and bring to the boil.

Reduce to a simmer, place a lid on the pan, and cook for 15 minutes.

Remove from the heat, add the lemon zest and fresh coriander. Stir well. Remove the cardamoms from the dish.

Serve with chapattis or rice.

Sweet Potato and Peas

Preparation time 30 minutes, cooking time 70 minutes

SERVES 4-6

700 g sweet potatoes, peeled and diced into 3 cm chunks
100 g frozen peas

KEY SPICES
1 tsp cumin seeds
1 tsp coriander seeds
¼ tsp black peppercorns

1 1inch piece of cassia bark
1 Indian bay leaf

½ tsp turmeric powder
1 tsp red chilli flakes

WARMING SPICES
1 tbs fenugreek leaves, soaked in 2tbs hot water

OTHER SPICES
½ tsp asafoetida
1 tsp mango powder

WET INGREDIENTS
4 tbs vegetable oil
1 large onion, finely chopped
150 g chopped tomatoes
2 tsp pulped garlic
2 tsp pulped ginger
2-3 fresh green chillies, pierced
80 ml water

1 small bunch coriander chopped, including stalks
1 tsp jaggery
Himalayan pink rock salt to taste

Pre heat the oven to gas mark 6, 400°F (200°C).

Place the sweet potatoes in a baking tray, add 2 tbs of oil and salt to taste, then toss the potatoes to ensure that the oil coats all of the potatoes. Bake for 20 minutes.

Remove and chop the stalks from the fresh coriander, and set aside.

Take a small dry frying pan, set on a low heat, and warm through the cumin seeds, coriander seeds and black peppercorns until fragrant. This should take 1 minute, as you are just trying to tease the oil out of the spices. Remove from the heat, add to the pestle and mortar and grind coarsely.

Take a large sauté pan, add 2 tbs of the oil and warm on a low heat. Then add the asafoetida, onion, cassia bark and Indian bay leaf. Sauté for 5 minutes.

Add the turmeric powder and red chilli flakes, stir and sauté for 2 minutes.

Add the mango powder, chopped tomatoes, coriander stalks, jaggery and salt to taste, and continue to sauté for a further 10 minutes, stirring occasionally.

By cooking these ingredients for a little longer, your curry will definitely taste better.

Now add the garlic, ginger and green chillies, and sauté for 2 minutes.

Add the contents of the pestle and mortar, stir well, and sauté for about 10 minutes, until you see that the mixture resembles a paste.

If the paste becomes a little dry and sticks to the pan, then just add a little water whenever you need, to help you achieve the required consistency.

Add 80 ml of water and the baked sweet potatoes, reduce the heat to medium, cover the pan and cook for 10 minutes, adding a splash of water if anything starts to stick to the bottom of the pan.

Add the peas and fenugreek leaves and cook uncovered for 3 minutes, or until the peas are cooked.

Garnish with the fresh coriander leaves.

Sweet potatoes have a creamy texture and a flavour which makes them ideal for Indian dishes.

They are rich in fibre, vitamins A, C and B6, and are a really good source of carbohydrates. I have added a little asafoetida, otherwise known as hing, to this dish. It delivers a flavour that I think is incredible and it provides calcium, phosphorous, iron, niacin, carotene and riboflavin.

Egg Curry

Preparation time 15 minutes,
cooking time 45 minutes.

SERVES 4-6

Six fresh medium size eggs, boiled for 8
minutes, with the shells removed, and 4
slits made on the outside of each egg.

KEY SPICES
1 tsp cumin seeds
1 tsp coriander seeds
1 tsp brown mustard seeds

1 Indian bay leaf
1 1 inch piece of cassia bark

½ tsp turmeric powder
1 tsp red chilli flakes

WARMING SPICES
6 green cardamoms, lightly bashed
2 cloves
1 tsp fenugreek leaves, soaked in 2 tbs
hot water

WET INGREDIENTS
2 tbs coconut oil
2 medium size onions, chopped finely
3 medium sized fresh tomatoes, finely
chopped
1 tsp pulped garlic
1 tsp pulped ginger
2 fresh green chillies, pierced
1 tbs fresh grated coconut (frozen is fine)
250 ml hot water
1 tbs tamarind pulp

1 tsp grated jaggery
Sea salt or rock salt to taste

TO GARNISH
Small bunch of fresh coriander, chopped
Zest of one small fresh lime

Take a small frying pan, set on a low heat, and warm through the cumin seeds, coriander seeds and black peppercorns until fragrant.

This should only take 1 minute. It is important that this is done gently, as you need to just tease the oil out of the spices. You need the spice flavours to enhance the onions.

Add to the pestle and mortar, and coarsely grind.

Heat the coconut oil in a large sauté pan, add the Indian bay leaf and cassia bark. Then stir in the onions, and sauté for 5 minutes.

Add the turmeric powder and red chilli flakes, and continue to sauté for a further 5 minutes

Add the tomatoes, jaggery and sea salt to taste. Stir and continue to cook until the oil begins to appear on the surface, or separates from the onions and tomatoes after about 10 minutes

Add the contents of the pestle and mortar, as well as the garlic, ginger and green chillies. Cook for at least 3 minutes.

Add the grated coconut, and cook for a further 1 minute.

Add the water, bring to the boil and immediately reduce to a simmer.

Add the eggs, tamarind pulp, green cardamoms, cloves and soaked fenugreek leaves. Place the lid on the pan and simmer for 15 minutes.

Remove from the heat, and stir in the fresh coriander and lime zest.

Serve with fresh chapattis

You can add some fine green beans to this egg curry if you like. Just add to the dish at the same time as the eggs.

Remember to count your cardamoms and cloves in and count them out again before serving.

Such a humble dish, and loaded with protein from the eggs. I make it with coconut oil and I use jaggery instead of sugar. Jaggery plays an important role in many of my dishes, balancing out the natural acidity of the tomatoes.

Black-Eyed Peas
with Lime Pickle

Preparation time 30 minutes,
cooking time 90 minutes.
Overnight soaking.

It's best to use dry black-eyed peas, and
these need to be soaked overnight.

SERVES 4

150g black-eyed peas
900 ml water

KEY SPICES
1 tsp cumin seeds
1 tsp coriander seeds
½ tsp brown mustard seeds
½ tsp black peppercorns

1 1 inch piece of cassia bark
1 Indian bay leaf

½ tsp turmeric powder
1 tsp red chilli flakes

WARMING SPICES
1 star anise

OTHER SPICES
1 tsp asafoetida

WET INGREDIENTS
3 tbs vegetable oil
1 large onion, finely chopped
250 g good quality chopped tinned
tomatoes
1 tbs Indian lime pickle
1 fresh finger green chilli, pierced

1 tsp jaggery
Rock salt or salt flakes to taste
Small bunch of fresh coriander, roughly
chopped
Zest of one lemon
Juice of half a lemon

Soak the black-eyed peas overnight.

Take the soaked black-eyed peas and wash thoroughly.

Add the black-eyed peas and 900ml of water to a large saucepan, bring to the boil, add the asafoetida, immediately reduce the heat to a simmer, then place the lid on the pan and cook for 35 minutes, or until the peas are tender. You should be left with some water in the saucepan.

Take a small dry frying pan, set on a low heat, and warm through the cumin seeds, coriander seeds, brown mustard seeds, black peppercorns and star anise, and warm through until fragrant. This should take 1 minute, as you are just trying to tease the oil out of the spices.

Remove from the heat, remove the star anise and place this to one side. Pour the remainder of the spices into a pestle and mortar, and grind coarsely.

Take a large sauté pan, add the oil and warm on a low heat. Then add the onion, cassia bark and bay leaf. Sauté for 5 minutes.

Add the turmeric powder and red chilli flakes, stir and sauté for 2 minutes.

Add the chopped tomatoes, lime pickle, green chilli, jaggery and salt to taste, and continue to sauté for a further 10 minutes, stirring occasionally.

By cooking these ingredients for a little longer, your curry will definitely taste better.

Add the contents of the pestle and mortar, stir well, and sauté for about 10 minutes, until you see that the mixture resembles a paste.

If the paste becomes a little dry and sticks to the pan, then just add a little water whenever you need, to help you achieve the required consistency.

Add the black eye peas, stir well, and then add the star anise.

Place the lid on the pan and gently simmer for 20 minutes (add a little more water if the peas appear a little dry).

Remove from the heat, add the chopped coriander, lemon zest, and lemon juice. Stir and allow to sit for 5 minutes before serving.

Chana Dal with Tamarind and Tomatoes

Preparation time 30 minutes, cooking time 2 hours.

SERVES 4

250g chana dal
900 ml water

KEY SPICES
1 tsp cumin seeds
1 tsp brown mustard seeds
1 tsp red chilli flakes
½ tsp turmeric powder
2-3 cm piece of cassia bark
1 tsp crushed coriander seeds
¼ tsp crushed black peppercorns
1 Indian bay leaf

OTHER SPICES
1 tsp asafoetida
2 tbs tamarind pulp

WARMING SPICES
1 heaped teaspoon of fenugreek leaves, soaked in 2 tbs of hot water

WET INGREDIENTS
2 tbs clarified butter (or vegetable oil)
2 tsp pulped garlic
2 tsp pulped ginger
4 large ripe tomatoes, finely chopped
1 tsp tomato purée
1 tsp grated jaggery
1 tbs natural yogurt
3 whole green chillies, pierced on both sides
1 tsp sea salt or rock salt
One small bunch of fresh coriander, roughly chopped
Zest and juice of a small lime

TEMPERING (OPTIONAL)

2 tsp groundnut oil
½ tsp brown mustard seeds
½ tsp cumin seeds
6 curry leaves
1 dry Kashmiri red chilli

Wash and add the lentils to a large pan containing 900ml of water, and bring to the boil. Reduce to simmer and skim off any starch or froth that appears on the surface with a spoon.

Add ½ tsp of asafoetida, place the lid on the pan and simmer, stirring regularly, for 45 -50 minutes.

Remove the lentils from the heat and gently give them a light mash. If the lentils seem a little dry, add some more water, and then set aside.

Place the clarified butter in a cold saucepan, and gently heat on a low heat. Then add all of the key spices and the remaining ½ tsp of asafoetida. Warm through for 50 seconds.

Add the garlic and ginger, saute for 5 minutes, then add the tomatoes, tomato puree and jaggery.

Cook and reduce down for 10 minutes, then remove the pan from the heat and allow to cool for one minute.

Stir in the yogurt really well, add the green chillies, and bring the pan back to the boil. Then, immediately reduce to a low heat, cooking out the yogurt for 5 minutes

Add the soaked fenugreek leaves and stir. Take the saucepan and add the contents to the lentils, stirring really well. Add the tamarind pulp, and simmer for 15 minutes with the lid on. If the lentils become quite thick you can just add a little more water to loosen them up.

Remove from the heat. Season to taste with salt and add the fresh coriander, lime zest and lime juice.

If it's a special occasion, why not temper the dal just before taking it to the table. To do this, simply heat the groundnut oil, in a small pan, on a medium heat. Add the brown mustard seeds and allow them to splutter. Then add the cumin seeds allowing them to sizzle, pop in the curry leaves and red chillies. Once the curry leaves start to splutter, pour the whole mixture over the lentils.

Lemon and Lime Rasam

Preparation time 30 minutes, cooking time 70 minutes

SERVES 4

150 g toor lentils (pigeon peas)

KEY SPICES
½ tsp cumin seeds
½ tsp coriander seeds
½ tsp brown mustard seeds

½ tsp turmeric powder
1 tsp red chilli flakes

WARMING SPICES
½ tsp fennel seeds
2 dry Kashmiri chillies
6 fresh curry leaves
1 tsp fenugreek leaves

WET INGREDIENTS
2 tbs vegetable oil
1 tsp pulped garlic
1 tsp pulped ginger
2 fresh finger green chillies, slit lengthways
2 fresh tomatoes, chopped
450 ml warm water
1 tbs fresh lime juice
1 tbs fresh lemon juice

1 tsp jaggery
Sea salt or salt flakes to taste
Small bunch of coriander, chopped coarsely

Wash and soak the lentils for 30 minutes.

Bring the lentils to the boil in the water they have been soaking in, in a saucepan, and simmer with the lid on for 30 minutes, or until the lentils are soft and mushy and all the water has been absorbed.

In a small dry frying pan set on a low heat, except for the turmeric powder and chilli flakes, place all the key spices and warming spices in the pan and very gently warm through for 1 minute.

Remove from the heat, place in a pestle and mortar, and grind to a powder. Set aside.

In a deep heavy pan, heat the oil gently, add the garlic, ginger, turmeric powder, red chilli flakes and green chillies, ensuring that the heat is set to low. Gently fry for 1 minute.

Add the tomatoes, jaggery and salt to taste, then add the key spices from the pestle and mortar and cook for a further 10 minutes. You can add a little water if you need to.

Add the mashed lentils to the pan together with 450 ml of warm water, bring to the boil and then reduce to a simmer for 10 minutes.

Add the lemon and lime juice, and switch off the heat. Cover with a lid for 5 minutes.

Remove the lid, add the fresh coriander, and serve with plain steamed rice, or just drink it on its own.

My Dad used to make this recipe if any of us had a cough or cold, and I now make it for my own family. I use pigeon peas, which are an excellent source of fibre, protein and sodium. They are low in fat, and are considered an ideal food for heart-healthy diets. You can simply pour this into a large mug and sip it on its own – a natural cure for a blocked nose and tickly throat.

Red Adzuki Beans

Preparation time 30 minutes,
cooking time 80 minutes

SERVES 4

150 g Adzuki beans
850 ml of water

KEY SPICES
1 tsp cumin seeds
1 tsp coriander seeds, crushed
½ tsp brown mustard seeds
¼ tsp black peppercorns, crushed
1 tsp red chilli flakes

WARMING SPICES
3 cloves
4 green cardamoms, lightly bashed

OTHER SPICES
1 tsp asafoetida

WET INGREDIENTS
4 tbs clarified butter
3 banana shallots, finely chopped
2 large ripe tomatoes, finely chopped
1 tsp naga chilli paste
2 tsp pulped garlic
1 tsp pulped ginger
juice of ½ a lime

1 tsp grated jaggery
6 fresh curry leaves
1 small bunch of coriander including the
stalks, chopped

Wash the Adzuki beans and place in a large saucepan. Add the water and bring to the boil. Add the asafoetida and reduce to a simmer, with the lid on, for about 40 minutes, or until the beans are nice and tender.

In a frying pan, add the clarified butter and warm very gently on a low heat. Add all the key spices and warming spices, and allow to warm through for 1 minute.

Remove the cloves and green cardamoms and set aside.

Add the shallots to the frying pan, and sauté for 10 minutes.

Add the cloves, green cardamoms, tomatoes, naga paste, garlic, ginger, and jaggery, stirring really well, and cook for at least 10 minutes.

Add the lime juice and the curry leaves, stirring really well.

Add to the Adzuki beans, stir and simmer on a very low heat for 10 minutes.

Remove from the heat, add fresh coriander, and serve with chapattis.

Remember to count your cardamoms in and count them out again before serving.

Red adzuki beans carry the flavor of the blend of spices really well. Adzuki beans are a great element of a diabetic diet plan to help treat, manage or prevent diabetes. They are very tasty and are one of the most antioxidant rich foods you will find.

Red Lentils and Yellow Split Peas with Coconut Milk

Preparation time 30 minutes, cooking time 80 minutes

SERVES 4-6

150 g red split lentils (masoor dal)
150 g yellow split peas

KEY SPICES
1 tsp cumin seeds
1 tsp coriander seeds
1 tsp brown mustard seeds
¼ tsp black peppercorns

1 1 inch piece of cassia bark
1 Indian bay leaf

1 tsp turmeric powder
1 tsp sweet smoked paprika

WARMING SPICES
2 cloves
4 green cardamoms, lightly bashed
1 black cardamom, lightly bashed

WET INGREDIENTS
1.5 litres water
2 tsp pulped ginger
3 tbs coconut oil
1 large onion, diced finely
2 tsp pulped garlic
2 tsp sundried tomato paste
200 ml coconut milk
2 tbs tamarind pulp

6-8 fresh curry leaves (optional, but try to get hold of them if you can)
Sea salt to taste

GARNISH
1 small bunch of coriander including the stalks, chopped
Zest of one small lime

Wash the lentils and split peas thoroughly until the water runs clear, then place them in a large saucepan with the water.

Bring to the boil, then immediately reduce to a simmer, add 1 tsp pulped ginger, cover and simmer for about 30-40 minutes.

Whilst the lentils and split peas are simmering, take a small dry frying pan on a low heat, add the cumin seeds, coriander seeds, brown mustard seeds and black peppercorns, and gently warm for 1 minute. Remove from the pan, add to a pestle and mortar, grind to a fine powder and set aside.

In the same pan, set on a low heat, add the warming spices and gently warm for 1 minute. Then remove from the heat and leave in the pan on one side.

Place a sauté pan on a low heat, add the coconut oil and allow to warm, then add the curry leaves and allow to splutter.

Add the chopped onions, cassia bark and Indian bay leaf, and sauté for 5 minutes.

Add turmeric powder, paprika and salt to taste. Turn the heat to medium and sauté the onions until a light golden-brown colour.

Add the garlic, 1 tsp of the ginger, sundried tomato paste and the contents of the pestle and mortar, and continue to cook until the oil begins to separate from the onions after about 10 minutes. If the mixture becomes a little dry and sticks to the pan, simply add a little water.

Remove from the heat and add to the simmering lentils along with the coconut milk, tamarind pulp and warming spices.

Simmer uncovered for about 20 minutes. The lentils should begin to thicken, but at this stage you can adjust to how you would prefer the lentils. This recipe should give a relatively thick consistency, but if your preference is for the lentils to be a little more 'soupy' you can add a touch more water.

Remove from the heat, add the chopped coriander and lime zest, stir well and add sea salt to taste if required. Remove the cardamoms and cloves.

Allow the lentils to sit for 5 minutes before serving with rice or chapattis

These lentils are mild and geared towards introducing children to spice. If you would like a bit more spice, take a few ladles of the finished dish, add to a small pan, split a green chilli and just simmer for a minute or two.

This is a great dish to introduce your children to lentils. If I am catering for an event and there are children to consider, I often add this to the menu. The children always love it.

Tarka Dal

Preparation time 40 minutes, cooking time 75 minutes.

SERVES 4

300 g red split lentils
1 litre cold water

KEY SPICES
½ tsp cumin seeds
1 tsp coriander seeds
1 tsp brown mustard seeds
¼ tsp black peppercorns

1 Indian bay leaf
1 1 inch piece of cassia bark

½ tsp turmeric powder
1 tsp red chilli flakes

WARMING SPICES
2 tsp fenugreek leaves, soaked in 4tbs hot water

WET INGREDIENTS
2 tbs vegetable oil
2 oz clarified butter
2 tbs tamarind pulp
2 tbs good creamy natural yogurt
1 large onion, finely chopped (even better if you can purée the onion in a blender)
200 g good quality tinned chopped tomatoes
2 tsp pulped garlic
1 tsp pulped ginger
2-3 fresh green chillies, pierced (the number of chillies should reflect your preferred level of heat)

1 tsp grated jaggery
Sea salt to taste
Small bunch of fresh coriander, chopped

FOR THE TEMPERING
1 tbs groundnut oil
6-8 fresh curry leaves
1 tsp brown mustard seeds
½ tsp cumin seeds
1 garlic clove, cut into fine slithers
2 dry red Kashmiri chillies

Soak the lentils in hot water for at least 30 minutes. Then drain, and wash thoroughly under a cold running tap, until the water runs clear.

Bring the lentils to the boil in 1 litre of cold water, over a high heat.

You will notice that some foam appears on the surface. This is just starch, but for a cleaner finish remove this with a slotted spoon.

Reduce the heat to a simmer for 20 minutes, or until the lentils are tender.

Drain half of the water from the lentils, and set the lentils aside.

Once the lentils are cooled, stir in the tamarind pulp and yogurt.

In a dry frying pan gently warm through the cumin seeds, coriander seeds, mustard seeds and black peppercorns, over a low heat for 1 minute until fragrant. Add to a pestle and mortar, and grind coarsely.

Take a large sauté pan add the oil, butter, Indian bay leaf, cassia bark and warm through on a low heat. Add the onion and fry until translucent and light brown. This will take at least 10 minutes.

Add the turmeric powder and red chilli flakes, and sauté for a further 2 minutes

Add the chopped tomatoes and jaggery, and cook for a further 10 minutes, or until you see the oil begin to appear at the sides or on the surface of the onions and tomatoes.

Add the spices from the pestle and mortar, stir really well and cook for 2 minutes.

Add the garlic, ginger and green chillies. Cook for a further 2 minutes, and season with sea salt.

Add the contents of the sauté pan to the lentils, stir well, and bring the lentils back to the boil.

Reduce immediately to a gentle simmer, add the soaked fenugreek leaves, and cook for 10 minutes, or until you have the lentils to the thickness you like to eat them.

Now for the secret to making the best tasting lentils. It really is all about the tempering.

Heat the groundnut oil in a small frying pan, add all the remaining tempering ingredients, and fry for 30 seconds.

Remove from the heat, and pour the tempering ingredients over the cooked lentils.

Add fresh coriander, and serve with boiled rice or chapattis

Red Kidney Bean and Sweet Potato Patties

Preparation time 30 minutes, cooking time 90 minutes

SERVES 4

250 g cooked canned kidney beans
1 large sweet potato, roasted and with the flesh removed

KEY SPICES
½ tsp turmeric powder
1 tsp red chilli flakes

1tsp cumin seeds
1tsp coriander seeds

WARMING SPICES
2 green cardamoms

OTHER SPICES
2 tsp mango powder
¼ tsp ajwain seeds
¼ tsp asafoetida

WET INGREDIENTS
2 tbs good natural yoghurt
1 tsp mango pickle, ground in a pestle and mortar
1 tbs freshly grated coconut (frozen is fine)
2 tbs coconut oil (or vegetable oil)
1 onion, finely chopped
1 tsp pulped garlic
1 tsp pulped ginger
1 green chilli, finely chopped
2 tsp sundried tomato paste
Small bunch of coriander, roughly chopped
1 tbs fresh lemon juice
Zest of one small lemon

Pinch of sea salt

2 large eggs, whisked
50 g plain flour
200 g breadcrumbs (you can make the crumbs from chapattis)
Groundnut oil for shallow frying

Rinse and drain the kidney beans. Place them on a clean tea towel to absorb most of the moisture. Then place them in a bowl, stir in the mango powder, yogurt, mango pickle, turmeric powder and red chilli flakes. Add a pinch of sea salt. Stir really well. Set aside.

Place a small dry frying pan on a low heat, and warm the cumin seeds, coriander seeds, green cardamoms and ajwain seeds for 1 minute.

Remove from the heat, place in the pestle and mortar, give the green cardamom a little bashing, and remove the seeds. Place the seeds back into the mortar, and discard the husk

Roast the grated coconut in the same pan until a light golden-brown colour, add to the pestle and mortar along with the garlic, ginger, green chilli and sundried tomato paste. Grind to a smooth paste. Set aside.

Place the oil in a large sauté pan, warm through on a low heat, add the asafoetida, stir and allow to sizzle for a few seconds.

Add the onions and fry until golden-brown, this should take about 7-8 minutes.

Add the contents of the pestle and mortar into the sauté pan, stir really well, and add 2 or 3 tablespoons of water to help the spices infuse into the wet ingredients.

Remembering that the heat should still be set to low, cook these ingredients until you get something which resembles a paste.

If the paste becomes a little dry and sticks to the pan, then just add a little water whenever you need, to help you achieve the required consistency.

Add the kidney beans and roasted sweet potato, stir really well, turn the heat up to medium and cook for 5-6 minutes. Remove from the heat, add the chopped coriander, lemon juice and lemon zest. Stir, gently mash a little and leave to cool.

Once cooled, divide the mixture into small balls, and then shape into patties. Whisk the eggs in one bowl, with the flour in a second bowl, and the breadcrumbs in a third bowl.

Place the patties in the flour and lightly cover. Then place in the egg, and then in the breadcrumbs.

Place the patties in the fridge for at least 30 minutes.

Remove from the fridge, heat the oil and shallow fry the patties until golden-brown.

Remove and place on absorbent paper.

Serve with mint and coriander raita.

Lentils with Limes

Preparation time 20 minutes, cooking time 60 minutes

SERVES 4

250g masoor daal (red lentils - not sure why they are labelled red lentils, when clearly they are orange!)

KEY SPICES
1 tsp cumin seeds
1 tsp brown mustard seeds
1 tsp coriander seeds

1 tsp cayenne powder (or red chili flakes)
1 tsp turmeric powder

WARMING SPICES
2 black cardamoms, lightly bashed

OTHER SPICES
Pinch of asafoetida

WET INGREDIENTS
2 tbs vegetable oil
1 oz unsalted butter
2 medium onions, finely diced
2 medium sized ripe tomatoes, chopped finely
2 tsp pulped garlic
1 tsp pulped ginger
3 fresh green chillies, pierced
Juice of two fresh limes

Sea salt to taste
1 tsp grated jaggery

GARNISH
Small bunch of fresh coriander, chopped
Zest of two limes

Wash the lentils several times until the water runs clear, then place in a large saucepan with water and a pinch of asafoetida. Bring to the boil.

Skim away the foam as the lentils begin to boil, then reduce to a simmer for about 20 minutes. The lentils should be very soft.

Place a small dry frying pan on a low heat. Except for the cayenne pepper and turmeric powder, place all the key spices in the pan and gently warm through for 1 minute.

Remove from the heat, place in a pestle and mortar, grind to a powder and set aside.

Place a sauté pan on a medium-low heat, add the oil and butter, and allow to warm.

Add the onions and salt to taste, and sauté for 5 minutes.

Add the cayenne pepper and turmeric powder, turn the heat to medium and sauté for 5 minutes until the onions are a light golden-brown colour.

Add the tomatoes, garlic, ginger, green chillies, jaggery, contents of the pestle and mortar, and black cardamoms. Stir and reduce the heat to low.

Sauté for about 10-12 minutes until you have something that looks like a paste. Add a little extra water if the mixture starts to stick to the pan.

Add the cooked lentils and lime juice, and season with a little more salt if needed.

Place a lid on the pan and simmer for 5 minutes. If the lentils seem a little thick, loosen with a little water.

Remove from the heat and add fresh coriander and lime zest.

Serve with rice or chapattis

Remember to count your cardamoms in and count them out again before serving.

I have always loved making these lentils, which are one of the most common varieties used in Indian food. My Dad used to make these every other week, and we always had lots of varieties of lentils in our cupboards. I am surprised that many people only ever use one or two varieties. In our cooking school we use over 25 different types of lentils.

Roasted Chickpea Flour with Yogurt

Preparation 30 minutes, cooking time 30 minutes

SERVES 4

50 g sifted chickpea flour (gram flour)
200 ml natural yogurt

KEY SPICES
1 tsp turmeric powder
1 tsp red chilli flakes
½ tsp cumin seeds
½ tsp crushed coriander seeds
1 Indian bay leaf
1 1 inch piece of cassia bark

WARMING SPICES
1 tsp fenugreek leaves, soaked in 2 tbs of hot water

OTHER SPICES
½ tsp asafoetida
2 whole dry red chillies

WET INGREDIENTS
1 litre of cold water
2 tbs groundnut oil
1 tsp pulped garlic
1 tsp pulped ginger
1-2 fresh green chillies, pierced

6 fresh curry leaves (optional)
1 tsp grated jaggery
Salt flakes to taste
1 small bunch of fresh coriander, roughly chopped

Heat a dry frying pan on a low heat, add the chickpea flour and roast for 3 minutes, stirring continuously. Do not leave unattended, as the flour will burn.

Remove from the heat and allow to cool.

Place the yogurt in a large bowl along with the water, whisking together.

Add the turmeric powder, red chilli flakes, jaggery and salt flakes to the large bowl, and then stir in the roasted chickpea flour.

Heat the oil in a large sauté pan, on a low heat. Add the asafoetida, dry red chillies and the remaining key spices, sauté for 1 minute until fragrant.

Add the garlic, ginger and green chillies, and sauté for 1 minute.

Add the yogurt mixture, stirring well, and bring to the boil.

Reduce to a simmer, add the soaked fenugreek leaves and curry leaves, and cook for about 15 minutes.

Remove from the heat, and add the fresh coriander.

Serve immediately with plain boiled rice.

This is another dish that my Dad used to make whilst waiting for pay day. As children, money was very tight but we never went hungry, thanks to Dad's culinary wisdom. This recipe may sound a little odd, but it's an easy dish to make, and it's packed with flavour.

Toasted Husk Split Mung Beans with Raw Green Mango

Preparation time 30 minutes, cooking time 90 minutes

SERVES 4

150 g husk split mung beans
900 ml water

KEY SPICES
1 tsp cumin seeds
1 tsp coriander seeds
½ tsp brown mustard seeds
¼ tsp black peppercorns
1 1 inch piece of cassia bark
1 Indian bay leaf

1 tsp red chilli flakes
½ tsp turmeric powder

WARMING SPICES
5 green cardamoms, lightly bashed
1 black cardamom, lightly bashed

OTHER SPICES
½ tsp asafoetida
1 tsp mango powder

WET INGREDIENTS
4 tbs clarified butter (or vegetable oil)
2 banana shallots, finely chopped
2 tsp pulped garlic
1 tsp pulped ginger
4 large ripe tomatoes, chopped
1 red roasted pepper, chopped finely
1 small raw fresh green mango, peeled and grated
2-3 whole green chillies, pierced

1 tsp grated jaggery
Rock salt or sea salt to taste

GARNISH
Small bunch of coriander, roughly chopped
1 tbs fresh lemon juice

Lightly roast the mung beans in a dry skillet, and allow them to become golden-brown in colour.

Remove from the heat and allow to cool. Then wash thoroughly in a large sieve, under cold running water.

Place the mung beans in a large saucepan, add 900ml of water and bring to the boil. Immediately reduce to a gentle simmer, and remove any foam or starch from the surface with a slotted spoon.

Add the asafoetida, place the lid on the pan and allow to gently simmer for 30 minutes, or until the mung beans are soft. Remove from the heat and set aside.

Place a small dry frying pan on a low heat. Except for the turmeric powder and red chilli flakes, add the key spices and warming spices to the dry pan and warm through for 1 minute.

Remember you are only teasing the oil out of these spices, as you want the big hit of these spices whilst they are cooking in the onions.

Remove the cassia bark, bay leaf, green and black cardamoms. Set aside.

Add the remaining contents of the pan to a pestle and mortar, grind coarsely and set aside.

Place a large sauté pan on a low heat, add the butter, cassia bark and Indian bay leaf, and allow the butter to gently melt.

Add the shallots and gently sauté for 5 minutes.

Add the turmeric powder and red chilli flakes, and sauté for 1 minute.

Add the ginger and garlic, and sauté for 1 minute.

Add the chopped tomatoes, roasted pepper, jaggery and salt, and cook for a further 10 minutes.

Add the fresh mango, mango powder and green chillies. Cook for a further 5 minutes, then add the contents of the pan to the mung beans, stirring really well, and bring to the boil.

Reduce to a gentle simmer, place the lid on the pan, add the green and black cardamoms and simmer with the lid on for 15 minutes.

Remove from the heat, and add chopped coriander and lemon juice. Serve with boiled rice.

Remember to count your cardamoms in and count them out again before serving.

RICE & BREAD

This is the board which my Dad made for me. I used it from the age of 8 years old to roll out chapattis. Wearing my glass bangles, I worked out that it took 8 clicks of my bangles, then I turned the chapatti over, then another 8 clicks and there it was – a perfectly rolled chapatti.

Chickpea, Coconut and Mango Rice

Preparation time 20 minutes,
cooking time 45 minutes

SERVES 4

400 g basmati rice
800 g canned chickpeas, drained

KEY SPICES
1 tsp cumin seeds
1 tsp crushed coriander seeds
1/2 tsp crushed black peppercorns

WARMING SPICES
3 cloves
6 green cardamoms, bashed
1 black cardamom, bashed

WET INGREDIENTS
1 tbs coconut oil
2 onions, finely sliced
1 tbs tomato purée
2 tsp pulped garlic
1 tsp pulped ginger
1-2 tsp hot mango pickle
600 ml water
400 ml coconut milk

Himalayan pink rock salt to taste
1 small bunch coriander, roughly chopped
Natural yogurt, to serve

Wash the rice in a pan until the water runs clear, then leave the rice to soak in water for 30 minutes.

Heat the coconut oil in a large pan on a low heat, then add the key spices and warming spices, and fry until they begin to splutter. This should take 1 minute.

Add the onions, tomato puree, garlic and ginger and fry for 5 minutes.

Stir in the hot mango pickle and chickpeas, season with rock salt, and fry over a low-medium heat for 10 minutes.

Drain the rice in a colander, add to the sauté pan and fold and coat the rice with all the spices

Pour in the water, coconut milk and stir gently.

As soon as it comes to the boil, reduce the heat to a gentle simmer and cover tightly with a lid.

Simmer for 15-20 minutes or until all the excess liquid has been absorbed, and the rice is cooked.

Remove from the heat and stir in the fresh coriander.

Serve hot or at room temperature, with natural yogurt on the side.

Remember to count your cardamoms and cloves in and count them out again before serving.

Changing the grocer's sparkplugs was becoming a regular thing for Dad, and we invented this dish together when he came home with a box of mangoes after another successful mechanical intervention with the delivery van. Mangoes are great for helping you to keep healthy skin and hair. This is a wet rice dish, a little like a risotto.

Cumin Rice

Preparation time 10 minutes,
cooking time 20 minutes

SERVES 4

A really good guide when making rice is that for every one cup of rice, you need 2 cups of water.

300 g basmati rice

KEY SPICES
1 tsp cumin seeds
1 inch piece of cassia bark

WARMING SPICES
2 cloves
4 green cardamoms, lightly bashed

WET INGREDIENTS
2 tbs unsalted butter
2 onions, finely chopped
1 tsp pulped garlic
400 ml hot water

Melt the butter in a large pan, add the key spices and warming spices, and allow to sizzle for just 30 seconds.

Add the onions and fry for 5 minutes, and then add the garlic and fry for 5 minutes, stirring continuously.

Add the rice to the pan, stir well and pour over the 400 ml of hot water (or enough to cover the rice and leave an extra 2cm of water above the rice).

Bring to the boil, and boil until almost all of the water has evaporated. Reduce to the lowest simmer, place a kitchen paper towel over the rice, seal with the lid and simmer for 5 minutes.

Remove from the heat and do not touch the pan or remove the lid for 5 minutes. Then remove the lid and lift off the kitchen paper which should be quite wet.

Fluff the grains up with a fork and remove the cloves and cardamoms before serving.

Dad would usually make this rice when we had nothing much left in the cupboards. I have always found it really satisfying to eat on its own, as well as with a range of other dishes. You can add peas or most other vegetables, which you simply place on the rice before putting the kitchen paper on top of it.

Lamb Biryani

Part One - Biryani Rice

Preparation time for the biryani rice 30 minutes, cooking time 10 minutes

Serves 4

300 g basmati rice (I always use Tilda) washed and soaked in 250ml water

Key Spices
1 tsp cumin seeds

Warming Spices
3 green cardamoms, lightly bashed
2 black cardamoms, lightly bashed
2 cloves
¼ tsp freshly ground nutmeg
1 1 inch piece of cassia bark
1 Indian bay leaf

Wet Ingredients
2.3 litres of water
2 tbs clarified butter
1 tbs white wine vinegar

1 tsp sea salt

Place the rice in a large bowl and rinse under a running tap of cold water. Use your hands to turn the rice gently whilst the water is running. When the water begins to run clear, soak the rice in 250ml water for at least 30 minutes.

Place 2.3 litres of cold water in a large pan, bring to the boil and add all the spices to the water whilst it is still boiling. Then add the clarified butter, white wine vinegar and sea salt.

Before you add the rice to the water, ensure that you have a large clean tray with plenty of ice sitting under it. Don't worry all will be revealed soon.

Drain the soaked rice, then add it to the large pan and allow the rice to boil. Do not cover the rice and give it a very gentle stir.

Now this is the important bit - do not leave the pan and put on the timer or stopwatch from the point that the rice enters the large pan. It is exactly 4 minutes - no more and no less. This is a crucial step in making this iconic dish. What you are looking to achieve is to partly cook the rice.

Carefully drain the rice from the pan using a large colander.

Immediately spread the rice out onto the cold tray, using a fork to separate all the grains. This is to stop the cooking process. Some biryani recipes tell you to rinse the rice under cold water, but by doing that you rinse away a lot of the spices which you have added.

Remember to remove the cardamoms and cloves from the rice.

Once the rice is cold, you are on your way to making a biryani fit for a King!

Biryani is probably one of the most requested dishes at our cookery school. Some people are daunted by the biryani process, but like most things it just requires practice. One of the most important steps is getting the rice perfect, and that is why I have detailed this stage of the biryani recipe separately.

My Dad used to say that a good biryani is when the grains of rice fall separately onto your plate.

Marinate overnight.
Preparation time for the biryani 20 minutes,
cooking time 60 minutes

SERVES 4

500 g boneless shoulder of lamb, cut into
bite sized pieces

FOR THE MARINADE
1 tbs coriander seeds warmed and crushed
(you can use a pestle and mortar)
3 tsp pulped garlic
2 tsp pulped ginger
2 tbs raw papaya skin, grated (this is a
great tenderiser)
2 tbs chopped coriander stalks
1 tsp cumin seeds
2 tbs white wine vinegar
160 g natural yogurt
1 tsp turmeric powder
1 tsp red chilli flakes
1 tbs groundnut oil
4 green chillies (you can use less if you
want less heat)

FOR THE BIRYANI MASALA
1 tsp red chilli flakes
1 tsp turmeric powder
1 Indian bay leaf
1 1 inch piece of cassia bark
¼ tsp black peppercorns
2 tbs black cumin seeds (also known as
shahi jeera or kala jeera)
1 star anise
6 green cardamoms, lightly bashed
2 black cardamoms, lightly bashed
3 cloves
2 strands of mace
2 - 3 dry whole Kashmiri chillies
¼ tsp freshly ground nutmeg
1 tsp kalpasi* (optional - see footnote)

WET INGREDIENTS
3 large onions, sliced thinly
Sunflower oil for deep frying the onions
8 tbs clarified butter, melted
6-7 saffron threads, soaked in 140 ml of
semi-skimmed milk

GARNISH
Medium size bunch of coriander, chopped
Small bunch of mint, chopped
Juice and zest of 2 limes

1 medium sized onion, sliced and fried until
golden brown

Part Two – Making the Lamb Biryani

To marinate the lamb, take a large bowl and add all the marinating ingredients to the bowl. Mix well, then add the lamb and coat it with the marinade. Cover the bowl with cling film and leave to marinate in the fridge overnight.

Remove from the fridge and bring to room temperature for at least 20 minutes.

Place the lamb in an oven-proof dish and then put it in a pre-heated oven at 200 C, 400 F or gas mark 6 for 20 minutes. Remove from the oven and set aside.

Add all the biryani masala ingredients to a small pan and warm on a low heat for 1 minute. Add to a pestle and mortar, remove the husks from the green and black cardamoms and put the seeds back into the pestle and mortar Grind to a powder. Set aside.

Before deep-frying the onions, ensure that moisture is removed from the onions by putting them in a clean tea towel and gently squeezing them.

Then add the sunflower oil to a deep pan, heat to 380 C - 400 C (a small cube of bread turns light brown in 20 seconds) and fry the onions in batches to achieve an even golden-brown colour.

Carefully move the onions around gently in the oil and never leave the oil whilst doing this. Remove and drain the onions on absorbent kitchen paper. Set aside.

Chop the coriander and mint and mix together with the lime juice and zest. Set aside.

To layer the biryani, you will require a good heavy pan with a lid.

Before assembling the biryani, take a pastry brush and coat the bottom and sides of the pan with a little of the clarified butter to stop the rice from sticking.

Now you are ready to assemble all of the prepared ingredients.

This is the order which I build my biryani - the first layer is the biryani rice, followed by a sprinkling of saffron milk, a little of the clarified butter and some fried onions.

Then a layer of lamb followed by a sprinkling of the biryani masala, then the coriander, mint and lime.

Then repeat the layering again – biryani rice – saffron milk, clarified butter and onions – lamb - biryani masala – coriander, mint and lime.

I usually build two sets of layers, as described above.

Once the biryani has been assembled, seal the lid with some dough made with plain flour and water. Place the pan on a low heat for 25 minutes, then remove from the heat.

Garnish with fried onions and a little of the coriander, mint and lime.
Serve immediately.

*Kalpasi is a type of lichen which is scraped off the bark of trees and stones. It dries into dark brown flakes and adds a haunting earthy taste and lovely freshness to the dish.

Spinach and Coriander Rice

Preparation time 20 minutes, cooking time 30 minutes

SERVES 4

300 g basmati rice
500 g fresh spinach

KEY SPICES
1 Indian bay leaf
1 1 inch piece of cassia bark
1 tsp cumin seeds

WARMING SPICES
6 green cardamoms, lightly bashed
1 black cardamom, lightly bashed
2 cloves

WET INGREDIENTS
4 tbs clarified butter (vegetable oil if you prefer)
1 large onion, finely sliced
2 tsp pulped garlic
Stalks from a small bunch of coriander, chopped finely
600 ml water

Sea salt to taste

GARNISH
Small bunch of coriander leaves, chopped
Juice and zest of a small lime

Place the rice in a large bowl and wash under a cold tap until the water runs clear. Drain the rice and set aside.

Place a sauté pan on a low heat, add the clarified butter, and add the key spices and warming spices. Allow to sizzle for 1 minute.

Add the onion and sauté for about 6 minutes until a golden-brown colour.

Add the spinach, garlic, coriander stalks and sea salt to taste. Sauté until most of the water from the spinach has absorbed.

Add the rice and the water and bring to a vigorous boil. Continue to boil until most of the liquid has absorbed.

Then reduce to a very low simmer, carefully place a kitchen towel over the pan and secure by placing a lid on the pan.

Simmer for 5 minutes, switch off the heat and leave the pan covered for 10 minutes.

Take the lid off, fluff the rice with a fork, then add the fresh coriander, lime juice and zest. Fold in gently.

This rice is slightly wetter in its finished state than a normal rice.

Remember to count your cardamoms and cloves in and count them out again before serving.

This was another dish which Dad and I often made for unexpected guests, as we had spinach growing in our back garden. It's a relatively wet rice due to the spinach. It makes a great lunchtime meal, and for dinner goes really well with salmon.

Ajwain Seed Parathas

Preparation time 25 minutes, cooking time 15 minutes.

SERVES 4

250g chapatti flour, plus extra for dusting
¼ tsp sea salt (optional)
1 tsp ajwain seeds
5 tsp clarified soft butter
150 ml warm water

Sift the flour in a large bowl, add the sea salt, ajwain seeds and 1 tsp of the clarified butter. Mix into the flour with the tips of your fingers, then gradually add 150ml of warm water to form a soft dough.

Knead the dough for 5 minutes, or until you create a soft and smooth dough.

Divide the dough into six balls of equal size. Dust each ball with a little flour, and then roll out onto a surface. They should be 15cm in diameter.

Smear a little clarified butter on the dough. To create a triangle shape, first fold into a semi-circle, then fold the semi-circle in half again.

Place the triangle in a little flour, then roll it out gently into a larger triangle. Continue the same process with the remaining dough balls.

Heat the tawa (a flat disc shaped frying pan) to a medium-high heat, place one rolled out paratha on the tawa. After a few seconds you will notice small air pockets appearing in the dough. When this happens, flip the paratha over and brush with a little melted butter.

Gently press the paratha with a chapatti press, turning to cook the paratha on both sides for about 2 minutes.

Serve warm with your favourite lentils.

I remember rolling these parathas out on many Sunday mornings as a little girl. We sometimes used to eat them for brunch with leftover dishes from the evening before.

Spiced Loaves -
Baked in Tin Cans

Preparation time, rising and proving,
3 hours.
Cooking time 40-50 minutes.

330 g chapatti flour (chakki atta)
330 g stoneground wholemeal bread flour
6 clean empty tin cans

KEY SPICES
1 tsp cumin seeds
1 tsp coriander seeds, crushed
1 tsp red chilli flakes
½ tsp turmeric powder

WARMING SPICES
1 tsp fennel seeds
1 tsp dry fenugreek leaves

WET INGREDIENTS
60 g unsalted butter, with a little extra for
greasing
2 tbs honey
25 g fresh yeast
4 egg yolks
300 ml warm water

1 tsp sea salt flakes
1 beaten egg for egg wash

Sieve both of the flours into a bowl. Set aside.

Melt the butter and set aside, then place 1 tbs of honey and 4 tbs of warm water into a small bowl and mix really well.

Take the fresh yeast and crumble it over the honey and water. Stir only once and set aside.

Mix the melted butter with the contents of the small bowl. Then add the egg yolks, the remaining honey, 300 ml of warm water, key spices, warming spices and salt

Stir in half the flour and mix really well with your hands. Then add the remaining flour a little at a time. You should now begin to see a sticky dough. Turn the dough out onto a floured surface and sprinkle a little flour over the top of the dough.

Knead the dough for at least 15 minutes. Then grease a very large bowl with butter, place the kneaded dough into the bowl and cover loosely with cling film or a damp tea towel.

Rest the dough in a warm place for 2 hours.

Now take the raised dough, place it on a surface, knock out the air and cut into six equal parts.

Cover them with a damp cloth, then take each one and shape it into a loose ball, place inside a tin can and repeat until all the cans have been filled.

Cover the cans for a further 50 minutes, pre-heat the oven to 190°C / 375°F / gas mark 5, brush a little egg wash over the bread in each can and place in the oven for 40 to 50 minutes.

The bread should be really golden-brown when removed from the oven. Allow the cans to cool on a cooling rack.

The very first time I was taught to bake bread, it wasn't by my Dad, rather by my teacher Mrs Copperfield. Dad was impressed by the small loaf I brought home from school and soon decided that we should bake some at home. We didn't own any baking trays, so we used empty Fray Bentos tins or empty chickpea tins.

Chapattis

Preparation time 10 minutes, cooking time 2 minutes

MAKES 4 CHAPATTIS

100g wholemeal chapatti flour
A pinch of salt (optional)
1 tsp vegetable oil (optional)
50 ml lukewarm water

Salt and vegetable oil are optional in this recipe, as the food that you will eat the chapattis with should have enough salt and oil in already.

Sift together the flour and salt in a bowl. Stir in the vegetable oil and water, and then knead until firm. Shape into four round balls, coat with a little dry chapatti flour and roll out each ball into small rounds on a flat surface.

Heat the tawa. Cook the chapattis on both sides until golden brown, up to 1 minute per side.

Gluten-Free Lentil Bread

Preparation time 20 minutes, cooking time 30 minutes. Soak overnight.

150g urad daal (split black lentils)

KEY SPICES
1 tsp cumin seeds
Pinch of brown mustard seeds
1 tsp red chilli flakes

WARMING SPICES
1 tsp fenugreek leaves
1 tsp fennel seeds

WET INGREDIENTS
240ml water
1 small onion, chopped really finely
1 tsp pulped ginger
1 -2 fresh green chillies, minced (remove the seeds and membrane if you think it could be too hot for your liking)
Small bunch of fresh coriander with the stalks, chopped finely
3 tbs groundnut oil

½ tsp grated jaggery
Sea salt to taste

Wash and clean the lentils, then place in a large bowl and soak in water overnight.

Except for the red chilli flakes place the key spices and warming spices in a small dry frying pan on a low heat and roast for 1 minute.

Remove from the heat, add to a pestle and mortar, and grind to a powder. Set aside.

Drain the lentils and place them in a food processor along with the red chilli flakes, water, onion, ginger, green chillies, contents of the pestle and mortar, jaggery and sea salt to taste.

Pulverise in the food processor until you get a really smooth batter, which could take a few attempts.

Place the batter into a large bowl, and mix in the chopped coriander including the stalks. Stir well.

Place a skillet pan on a low heat, add a little oil, and tilt the skillet pan to ensure that you coat all of the pan's surface with the oil.

When the oil is at a medium but not a hot heat, add about 3 tbs of the batter and spread out with the back of a ladle to a diameter of about 20 cm (7-8 inches).

Cook for about 3 minutes then loosen the bread around the edges with a spatula or pallet knife. Flip, over and continue to cook for a further 3 minutes on the other side.

Serve warm with your favourite meat or vegetable curry.

Rumali Roti

Preparation time 60 minutes,
cooking time under 5 minutes

SERVES 4

220 g chapatti flour
55 g plain flour
Pinch of rock salt or salt flakes
250 ml cold water, as required
Rice flour, for dusting

Sieve the chapatti flour and plain flour into a large bowl. Add a pinch of salt to the flour, and gradually add cold water to make a soft dough.

Knead the dough for 5 minutes and then cover with a damp towel for 45 minutes. The dough should be very elastic.

After leaving for 45 minutes, knead again for 5 minutes.

Divide the dough into 8-9 equal portions. Shape them into round balls. Roll out each ball into small rounds on a surface covered with flour.

Hold the dough on the back of your palm and circle, twist and swing it. Continue until you get an even thickness and shape. The roti needs to be about 35 centimetres in diameter.

Cook the rotis on an upside down wok; they only take seconds to cook. Don't cook for too long, otherwise the rotis will become too dry and crispy.

Fold the roti into quarters and serve immediately.

'The word 'rumali' means handkerchief in many Indian languages, and 'rumali roti' means handkerchief bread. It is cooked on an upside-down tawa (Indian frying pan) or you could even use a wok. These thin breads are very nutritious and low in calories, as I don't cook them in ghee like some people do. One of the great things about rumali roti, compared to naan bread, is that the flavours of your food come through so much better because the roti is much lighter than a dense naan.'

CHUTNEY & PICKLES

I can't be without this saucepan, which
I have owned for over 40 years now.
Food always tastes better when I cook
in it. In 2013 I won a BBC Good Food
Bursary and made over 2,400 jars of my
'Route 207' marinade using this saucepan.

Burnt Aubergine and Tomato Chutney

Preparation time 20 minutes, cooking time 50 minutes

2 large aubergines
400 g of good quality tinned tomatoes

KEY SPICES
1 tsp cumin seeds
1 tsp brown mustard seeds
1 tsp turmeric powder
1 tsp red chilli flakes

WARMING SPICES
½ tsp nigella seeds
1 tsp fennel seeds
1 tsp fenugreek leaves, soaked in 2 tbs hot water

WET INGREDIENTS
2 tbs coconut oil (or vegetable oil if you prefer)
1 large brown onion, finely chopped
2 tsp sundried tomato paste
200 ml white wine vinegar
140 ml water
1 tsp pulped garlic
1 tsp pulped ginger

Sea salt to taste
200 g grated jaggery

Blacken the aubergines over a gas hob, (if you don't have a gas hob, put the aubergines under the grill) turning regularly with tongs, until completely charred and collapsed (you may wish to surround the rings with foil, as it can be messy). Allow to cool and mash in a bowl. Set aside.

Heat the oil in a large sauté pan on a medium heat.

Add the cumin seeds, mustard seeds and nigella seeds. Allow to sizzle, then add the onion, turmeric powder, chilli flakes and salt.

Sauté until the onions are golden-brown.

Add the aubergines, tomatoes, sundried tomato paste, white wine vinegar and jaggery.

Stir and continue to cook on a medium simmer for 10 minutes.

Add the water, fennel, fenugreek, garlic and ginger. Bring to the boil, and immediately reduce to a simmer. Place the lid on the pan, and cook for a further 20 minutes.

Remove from the heat when you are happy with the consistency of the chutney.

Allow to cool before placing in sterilised jars.

If you would like the chutney to be a little thicker, simply continue cook without the lid on for a little longer.

This is my favourite chutney. Dad and I would blacken the aubergines on the coals of an open fire in the back garden.

Hot Lemon Pickle

Preparation time 6 hours,
cooking time 10 minutes

2 lbs lemons
400 g grated jaggery

KEY SPICES
1 tbs cumin seeds
4 tbs brown mustard seeds

1 tsp turmeric powder
4 tbs red chilli flakes

WARMING SPICES
1 tbs fenugreek seeds
1 tbs fennel seeds
1 tbs nigella seeds

OTHER SPICES
1 tsp asafoetida

WET INGREDIENTS
1 tbs mustard oil (use vegetable oil if you prefer)
1 tsp pulped garlic
2 tsp pulped ginger

Sea salt

Wash and clean the lemons. Dry and remove the top and bottom of each lemon. Cut the lemons in half.

Try to remove most of the pips, place in a large bowl and sprinkle generously with sea salt.

Cover and leave for at least 6 hours, so that the juice can be drawn out from the lemons.

Allow the oil to warm in a large sauté pan on a low heat, add the asafoetida and stir for 10 seconds.

Add the cumin seeds, brown mustard seeds and the warming spices, stir and allow to warm through for 1 minute.

Carefully pour the juice from the bowl of lemons into the pan, add the jaggery and allow it to dissolve by gently stirring.

Bring the lemon juice mixture up to the boil, add the turmeric powder, red chilli flakes, garlic and ginger, then stir and cook for a further 1 minute.

Remove from the heat. When the mixture is cool, stir in the lemons, then pour into sterilised jars and keep at room temperature for at least 5 to 8 days, and then store in a cool dark place for at least 4 weeks before eating. I usually can't resist though, and start to eat before then!

It is the same process for making lime pickle, so just substitute limes for lemons in the above recipe

All the way through this book I have talked about my Dad's influence and recipes. However, pickles were my Mum's speciality. She would pickle just about anything, and even pickled the prized marrow which she grew in the front garden. Mr Mahi, our corner shop owner, used to let her have his used sweet jars, to store her pickles in. Dad used to tease her that Mr Mahi had the hots for her, which used to annoy her. I think that she really did have the hots for Detective Captain Steve McGarrett, the main character in the 1970s TV series Hawaii Five-0.

Fiery Mint Chutney

Preparation time 15 minutes,
cooking time 10 minutes

KEY SPICES
1 tsp cumin seeds
¼ tsp black peppercorns

WARMING SPICES
1 tsp fennel seeds

WET INGREDIENTS
100 ml water
1 tsp grated jaggery
4 tsp redcurrant jelly
2 tbs red wine vinegar
1 tsp pulped garlic
1-2 fresh green or red chillies, minced (or you can leave the chillies out altogether for a milder chutney)
1 large bunch of fresh mint, leaves picked and finely chopped
1 small bunch of coriander including the stalks, finely chopped

Sea salt to taste

Place a small dry pan on a low heat and gently warm through the key spices and warming spices for 1 minute.

Remove from the heat, place in a pestle and mortar, grind to a powder and set aside.

Take a small saucepan and bring the water, jaggery, redcurrant jelly and red wine vinegar up to the boil.

Remove from the heat, add the ground spices, garlic, chillies, mint, coriander and sea salt. Reduce to a simmer for 10 minutes.

Mix really well, cover and leave to cool before placing in a sterilised jar.

I absolutely adore this chutney. I grew up eating it with almost everything. I even used to put it on slices of green apple. Our neighbours used to give us the apples from the tree in their back garden.

Gooseberry and Ginger Chutney

Preparation time 10 minutes,
cooking time 30-40 minutes

450 g gooseberries

KEY SPICES
1 tsp cumin seeds
1 tsp red chilli flakes
1 tsp brown mustard seeds

WARMING SPICES
½ tsp nigella seeds
1 tsp fenugreek leaves
1 tsp fennel seeds

WET INGREDIENTS
2 large onions, finely chopped
570 ml white wine vinegar
450 g jaggery (or soft brown sugar)
1 tbs pulped ginger

4 tsp sea salt or to your taste

Gently cook the gooseberries in a little water until they have softened and are just starting to burst.

I can't give a precise time for this, it is best to 'judge by eye' on this one.

In the meantime take a small dry frying pan on a low heat, add the key spices and warming spices, and warm through for 1 minute.

Remove from the heat and add to the gooseberries.

Add the chopped onions, vinegar and salt, and cook for 10 minutes.

Add the jaggery and ginger, and boil gently until some of the liquid has evaporated, and the mixture has a slightly thicker consistency.

Cool slightly and put into sterilised jars.

This was a chutney which we created by accident in the first instance. In the very hot summer of 1976, our garden seemed to be overflowing with gooseberries. We used them to great effect, creating a range of new dishes.

Gooseberry Pickle

Preparation time 15 minutes,
cooking time 20-25 minutes

1 kg gooseberries

KEY SPICES
1 tsp cumin seeds
2 tsp brown mustard seeds
½ tsp turmeric powder
1 tsp red chilli flakes

WARMING SPICES
1 tsp fenugreek seeds
1 tsp fennel seeds
1 tsp nigella seeds

OTHER SPICES
1 tsp asafoetida

WET INGREDIENTS
350 ml water
170 ml sesame seed oil
6 whole red chillies
5 garlic cloves, chopped
5 tbs white wine Vinegar

4 tsp jaggery
12 fresh curry leaves, ripped into small pieces
1 tbs Himalayan pink rock salt

Simmer the gooseberries in the water and jaggery until they just begin to burst. Drain, stir in the salt and set aside (retain the drained water).

Heat the sesame oil on a low heat and add the key spices, warming spices, asafoetida, red chillies, garlic, and curry leaves and warm through gently.

Add to the gooseberries, mix well and sauté for 2 minutes. Then add the water drained from the gooseberries, bring to the boil and remove from the heat.

Allow the pickle to become lukewarm, and then add the vinegar. Stir really well.

Once cool, distil into sterilised jars.

This pickle became a neighbourhood favourite. We even convinced those gooseberry sceptics, like Ellen who lived opposite us, that they could enjoy these wonderful berries. The flavour of gooseberry varies, depending on a number of factors, from tart to sweet.

Rhubarb Chutney

Preparation time 15 minutes,
cooking time 25 minutes

500 g rhubarb, leaves removed, washed and sliced into fine chunks

KEY SPICES
1 tsp cumin seeds
1 tsp brown mustard seeds
¼ tsp turmeric powder
1 tsp red chilli flakes

WARMING SPICES
1 tsp fenugreek leaves
½ tsp fennel seeds

WET INGREDIENTS
1 medium banana shallot, finely chopped
100 ml white wine vinegar
1 tsp pulped ginger

200 g sugar
½ tsp salt flakes

In a dry pan, on a low heat, dry roast the key spices for 1 minute until fragrant. Set aside.

Heat the shallot, vinegar, ginger, sugar and salt in a non-aluminium pan. Bring to the boil for about 5 minutes, then add the rhubarb and the key spices in the warming pan.

Reduce the heat, and simmer for 15 minutes, then remove from the heat.

Place in a sterilised jar with the warming spices, while the chutney is still hot.

Lazy Chilli Flakes

Preparation time 10 minutes,
cooking time 5 minutes

50 g whole chillies, with stems removed (if
you like mild chillies, use Kashmiri)

KEY SPICE
Small pinch of black pepper

OTHER INGREDIENTS
15 ml white wine vinegar
3 tbs grated jaggery

Sea salt to taste

Place the white wine vinegar and jaggery in a sauté pan on a low heat, to gently dissolve the jaggery.

Grind the chillies in a pestle and mortar, or if you prefer you can use a food processor.

Add the ground chillies to the sauté pan, bring to the boil, remove from the heat and allow to cool in the pan.

Season with black pepper and sea salt.

Pour into a sterilised jar and store in the fridge.

I love having these to hand. I use them with omelettes, cheese on toast, or even a quick stir fry. My Dad used to make a large jar of these.

Peach and Roasted Shallot Chutney

Preparation time 20 minutes, cooking time 60 minutes

200 g shallots, peeled and halved, leaving the root end intact
300 g peaches, cut into wedges

KEY SPICES
1 tsp cumin seeds
2 tsp red chilli flakes
1 tsp brown mustard seeds
1/2 tsp black peppercorns

WARMING SPICES
1 tsp fennel seeds
1 tsp fenugreek leaves
1 tsp nigella seeds

WET INGREDIENTS
2 tbs vegetable oil
2 tsp pulped ginger
200 ml white wine vinegar
150 ml white wine

3 tbs brown sugar
Sea salt to season
200 g jaggery, broken into small chunks

Place the shallots in a large roasting tin with the oil and brown sugar, and roast at 200 C, 400 F or gas mark 6 for 30 minutes, or until the shallots have softened and caramelised. Please be careful not to burn them.

Remove and season with sea salt. Set aside.

Place a dry frying pan on a low heat, add all of the spices and gently warm through for 1 minute until fragrant.

Remove the pan from the heat, and coarsely grind the spices in a pestle and mortar. Set aside.

Place the peaches in a saucepan with a heavy base, along with the ginger, white wine vinegar, white wine and jaggery. Bring to the boil, then immediately reduce to a simmer for 10 minutes.

Stir in the shallots and the contents of the pestle and mortar, and simmer gently, stirring occasionally, for 10-15 minutes or until the chutney is nice and thick.

Whilst the chutney is still warm, add into sterilised jars.

Once you have tasted this chutney, you will always want a jar close to hand. It's incredibly versatile and goes with almost everything. I love cooking with shallots as they tend to be sweeter and milder than onions.

Roasted Almond
and Coriander Chutney

Preparation time 15 minutes,
cooking time 5 minutes

Large bunch of fresh coriander including
the stalks, chopped finely
50 g roasted almonds

KEY SPICES
1 tsp cumin seeds
1 tsp red chilli flakes

WARMING SPICES
½ tsp fennel seeds
½ tsp fenugreek leaves

OTHER SPICES
2 tsp mango powder

WET INGREDIENTS
1 tsp pulped garlic
2 tsp pulped ginger
1 small bunch fresh mint leaves, chopped
1 tbs grated jaggery (or brown sugar)
Juice and zest of half a lemon
1 tsp white wine vinegar
1 small mild red chilli, minced (optional)

Sea salt to taste

Place a dry frying pan on a low heat, and warm the key spices and warming spices for 1 minute. Transfer to a pestle and mortar or a blender.

Combine all of the ingredients in the pestle and mortar or blender. Grind or blend to your liking, to create a smooth or coarse chutney.

Store in a sterilised airtight jar in the fridge.

Almonds can be substituted with your choice of toasted nuts. For those of you with a nut allergy, this recipe works equally well with toasted chickpeas.

I still remember the first time Dad made this chutney in the back garden. It was a really warm evening, as usual we were all sat out in the back garden, and it began to rain. Dad wedged a huge plastic sheet between our kitchen window and our neighbour's fence. All the children and a couple of adults stood or sat under the sheet, whilst Dad ground the ingredients in my huge pestle and mortar. We ate the chutney with packets of Jacob's cream crackers.

Sweet Beetroot Chutney

Preparation time 15 minutes,
cooking time 30 minutes

2 large beetroots, grated
50 g freshly grated coconut (frozen is fine)

KEY SPICES
1 tsp cumin seeds
1 tsp brown mustard seeds
1 tsp red chilli flakes

WARMING SPICES
1 tsp fennel seeds
1 tsp fenugreek leaves
½ tsp nigella seeds

WET INGREDIENTS
2 tbs coconut oil
200 ml good quality coconut milk
140 ml water

6-8 curry leaves, ripped
25 g grated jaggery
Sea salt or rock salt to taste

Heat the oil in a large non-stick pan on a low heat. Add the key spices, warming spices and curry leaves, and gently warm for 1 minute until fragrant.

Add the beetroot, coconut, jaggery and salt to taste. Sauté for 5 minutes. Add the coconut milk and water, stir well and bring to the boil.

Reduce to a very low simmer, and cook until all of the liquid has absorbed, stirring occasionally. This should take about 20 minutes.

Remove from the heat, allow to cool, and serve with any of your favourite curries.

Beetroot is a truly amazing root vegetable. I have always loved its deep colour and its wonderful flavour. Having been a huge beetroot fan since the age of 4, I am convinced it has played a key role in keeping me wrinkle-free.

INDEX

GLOSSARY

Ajwain (seeds): Carom Seeds, Thyme, Caraway Seeds, Lovage Seeds

Aloo: Potato

Asafoetida: Very pungent spice extracted from the plant of the giant fennel family. Replaces garlic in many Indian dishes.

Basmati: Long grain rice from the Himalayan foothills

Biryani: Rice baked with meat or vegetables

Chana Dal: Cooked split Bengal Grams (split chickpeas)

Chapatti: Indian unleavened thin bread cooked on a griddle

Dabba: Spice container

Dal or Dhal: Pulse, lentil, legume, beans or dried peas

Dhansak: Chicken or meat dish cooked in a lentil puree

Dhungar, Tarka: Tempering (Tarka) with mustard seeds, cumin and garlic in hot oil

Ghee: Clarified butter

Gobi: Cauliflower

Jaggery: Solidified palm sugar or molasses

Keema: Minced meat curry

Kofta: Deep fried meat or vegetable balls

Mahi Mahi: a tropical firm white fish, also known as Dorade and available at most good supermarkets.

Masala: A mixture or blend of spices

Nigella seeds: Onion seeds

Pakora: Vegetable, meat or cheese coated in spicy chickpea batter and deep fried (similar to Bhaji but lighter).

Paneer: Indian cottage cheese

Paratha: Bread fried in butter on the griddle

Rasam: Gravy or juice

Rumali Roti: A very thin but large roti bread

Roti: General term for Indian unleavened bread

Tamarind: A date-like fruit used both in chutney and as a souring agent in cooking.

Tarka Dal: Cooked lentils garnished with tempered spices

Thoran: a dry, coconut based, chopped vegetable dish, briefly cooked over a high heat.

Oven temperatures

°C	Fan °C	°F	Gas	Description
110	90	225	¼	Very cool
120	100	250	½	Very cool
140	120	275	1	Cool
150	130	300	2	Cool
160	140	325	3	Warm
180	160	350	4	Moderate
190	170	375	5	Moderately hot
200	180	400	6	Fairly hot
220	200	425	7	Hot
230	210	450	8	Very hot
240	220	475	8	Very hot

Weights for dry ingredients

Metric	Imperial	Metric	Imperial
7g	¼ oz	425g	15oz
15g	½ oz	450g	1lb
20g	¾ oz	500g	1lb 2oz
25g	1 oz	550g	1¼lb
40g	1½oz	600g	1lb 5oz
50g	2oz	650g	1lb 7oz
60g	2½oz	675g	1½lb
75g	3oz	700g	1lb 9oz
100g	3½oz	750g	1lb 11oz
125g	4oz	800g	1¾lb
140g	4½oz	900g	2lb
150g	5oz	1kg	2¼lb
165g	5½oz	1.1kg	2½lb
175g	6oz	1.25kg	2¾lb
200g	7oz	1.35kg	3lb
225g	8oz	1.5kg	3lb 6oz
250g	9oz	1.8kg	4lb
275g	10oz	2kg	4½lb
300g	11oz	2.25kg	5lb
350g	12oz	2.5kg	5½lb
375g	13oz	2.75kg	6lb
400g	14oz		

Liquid measures

Metric	Imperial	Aus	US
25ml	1fl oz		
50ml	2fl oz	¼ cup	¼ cup
75ml	3fl oz		
100ml	3½fl oz		
120ml	4fl oz	½ cup	½ cup
150ml	5fl oz		
175ml	6fl oz	¾ cup	¾ cup
200ml	7fl oz		
250ml	8fl oz	1 cup	1 cup
300ml	10fl oz/½ pint	½ pint	1¼ cups
360ml	12fl oz		
400ml	14fl oz		
450ml	15fl oz	2 cups	2 cups/1 pint
600ml	1 pint	1 pint	2½ cups
750ml	1¼ pints		
900ml	1½ pints		
1 litre	1¾ pints	1¾ pints	1 quart
1.2 litres	2 pints		
1.4 litres	2½ pints		
1.5 litres	2¾ pints		
1.7 litres	3 pints		
2 litres	3½ pints		
3 litres	5¼ pints